Planning and Passing Your PhD De´

This book is a toolbox for PhD students to plan and prepare for the PhD defence regardless of their scientific discipline or location. The authors discuss various defence formats that are used internationally and identify the main differences and similarities.

With international examples, practical strategies, and tips from former PhD students and supervisors, this book unpacks the principles and unwritten rules underpinning the defence. Addressing planning and preparing for the doctoral defence, and what to do afterwards, this book covers topics such as:

- understanding your defence format
- preparing for committee questions
- preparing mentally and dealing with anxiety
- dealing with corrections, finalizing your graduation requirements and marking the end of your PhD trajectory.

This book is crucial reading for students across the world looking to defend their PhD thesis, and also for their supervisors and examiners.

Olga Degtyareva is an award-winning scientist turned productivity coach, who runs her own company, Productivity for Scientists, helping researchers around the world to be more productive and in charge of their day.

Eva O.L. Lantsoght is the Professor of Structural Engineering at the Universidad San Francisco de Quito, Ecuador, a tenured assistant professor at Technische Universiteit Delft, Netherlands, and author and co-host of the PhD Talk blog and podcast.

Insider Guides to Success in Academia

Series Editors:
Helen Kara,
Independent Researcher, UK and
Pat Thomson,
The University of Nottingham, UK.

The *Insiders' Guides to Success in Academia* address topics too small for a full-length book on their own, but too big to cover in a single chapter or article. These topics have often been the stuff of discussions on social media, or of questions in our workshops. We designed this series to answer these questions and to provide practical support for doctoral and early career researchers. It is geared to concerns that many people experience. Readers will find these books to be companions that provide advice and help to make sense of everyday life in the contemporary university.

We have therefore:

(1) invited scholars with deep and specific expertise to write. Our writers use their research and professional experience to provide well-grounded strategies to particular situations.
(2) asked writers to collaborate. Most of the books are produced by writers who live in different countries, or work in different disciplines, or both. While it is difficult for any book to cover all the diverse contexts in which potential readers live and work, the different perspectives and contexts of writers goes some way to address this problem.

We understand that the use of the term 'academia' might be read as meaning the university, but we take a broader view. Pat does indeed work in a university, but spent a long time working outside of one. Helen is an independent researcher and sometimes works with universities. Both of us understand academic – or scholarly – work as now being conducted in a range of sites, from museums and the public sector to industry research and development laboratories. Academic work is also often undertaken by networks which bring together scholars in various locations. All of our writers understand that this is the case, and use the term 'academic' in this wider sense.

These books are pocket sized so that they can be carried around and visited again and again. Most of the books have a mix of examples, stories and exercises as well as explanation and advice. They are written in a collegial tone, and from a position of care as well as knowledge.

Together with our writers, we hope that each book in the series can make a positive contribution to the work and life of readers, so that you too can become insiders in scholarship.

Helen Kara, PhD FAcSS,
independent researcher
https://helenkara.com/
@DrHelenKara (Twitter/Insta)
Pat Thomson PhD PSM FAcSS FRSA
Professor of Education, The University of Nottingham
https://patthomson.net
@ThomsonPat

Books in the Series include:

The Thesis by Publication in the Social Sciences and Humanities
Putting the Pieces Together
Lynn P. Nygaard and Kristin Solli

Your PhD Survival Guide
Planning, Writing and Succeeding in Your Final Year
Katherine Firth, Liam Connell, and Peta Freestone

Planning and Passing Your PhD Defence

A Global Toolbox for Success

Olga Degtyareva and Eva O.L. Lantsoght

LONDON AND NEW YORK

Cover image: © Getty Images

First published 2022
by Routledge
2 Park Square, Milton Park, Abingdon, Oxon OX14 4RN

and by Routledge
605 Third Avenue, New York, NY 10158

Routledge is an imprint of the Taylor & Francis Group, an informa business

© 2022 Olga Degtyareva and Eva O.L. Lantsoght

The right of Olga Degtyareva and Eva O.L. Lantsoght to be identified as authors of this work has been asserted in accordance with sections 77 and 78 of the Copyright, Designs and Patents Act 1988.

All rights reserved. No part of this book may be reprinted or reproduced or utilised in any form or by any electronic, mechanical, or other means, now known or hereafter invented, including photocopying and recording, or in any information storage or retrieval system, without permission in writing from the publishers.

Trademark notice: Product or corporate names may be trademarks or registered trademarks, and are used only for identification and explanation without intent to infringe.

British Library Cataloguing-in-Publication Data
A catalogue record for this book is available from the British Library

Library of Congress Cataloging-in-Publication Data
Names: Degtyareva, Olga, author. | Lantsoght, Eva O. L., author.
Title: Planning and passing your PhD defence : a global toolbox for success/ Olga Degtyareva and Eva O.L. Lantsoght.
Other titles: Planning and passing your PhD defense
Description: Abingdon, Oxon; New York, NY: Routledge, 2022. | Series: Insider guides to success in academia | Includes bibliographical references and index.
Identifiers: LCCN 2021024429 (print) | LCCN 2021024430 (ebook) | ISBN 9780367366650 (hardback) | ISBN 9780367366667 (paperback) | ISBN 9780429347900 (ebook)
Subjects: LCSH: Doctor of philosophy degree—Handbooks, manuals, etc. | Dissertations, Academic—Handbooks, manuals, etc.
Classification: LCC LB2369.D444 2022 (print) | LCC LB2369 (ebook) | DDC 378.2/42—dc23
LC record available at https://lccn.loc.gov/2021024429
LC ebook record available at https://lccn.loc.gov/2021024430

ISBN: 978-0-367-36665-0 (hbk)
ISBN: 978-0-367-36666-7 (pbk)
ISBN: 978-0-429-34790-0 (ebk)

DOI: 10.4324/9780429347900

Typeset in Helvetica
by codeMantra

Contents

1 Introduction: The PhD defence as the pinnacle of the PhD trajectory — 1
Scope — 2
Chapter structures — 5
How to use this book as a PhD student — 5
How to use this book as a supervisor — 6
How to use this book in a classroom setting — 8

2 Overview of defence formats — 13
History and purpose of the defence — 13
Defending before or after finalizing the thesis — 15
Written or oral defence — 17
Single-step versus two-step defences — 19
Public or behind closed doors — 21
Defence day – fixed schedules and schedules driven by committee — 22
Similarities and differences — 23
    Similarities — 23
    Originality — 25
    Differences — 27
Research results on doctoral defence practices and student perception — 29

3 Planning for a successful defence — 35
Overall planning of your PhD and possible pitfalls — 35
    The duration of a PhD program — 35
    Funding and the duration of your PhD — 39
    Sources of delays during the PhD — 40

	Hard deadlines for the PhD duration	45
	Planning towards your defence	46
	Working on your PhD with the defence in mind	51
	From research ideas to research planning	51
	Planning for different types of PhD programs	52
	Prepare for your defence by giving talks throughout your PhD	54
	Document your PhD journey	56
4	**Preparing for your defence**	**59**
	Preparing for all elements of your defence	59
	Elements of the defence	59
	Preparing to answer questions	61
	Practical aspects	61
	Research insights on preparing for the defence	62
	General preparation before the defence	67
	Our advice on preparing for the defence	67
	Former PhD candidates' experiences of preparing for the defence	69
	How committee members prepare for the defence	71
	Your committee	72
	Purpose of your committee	72
	Internal committee members	74
	External committee members	74
	Assigned committee	78
	Selecting a committee	79
	Preparing for committee feedback	82
	Making your presentation	82
	Presenting for your audience	82
	Summarizing your work	86
	Other forms of visual information	91
	Tips for presenting	92

	How to prepare for committee questions	95
	Dealing with anxiety before thesis submission and defence	101
	Dealing with anxiety before the thesis submission	102
	Dealing with anxiety before the thesis defence	104
	Practicing for the defence	109
5	**Defences around the world**	**115**
	Introduction	115
	The Netherlands	118
	Belgium	119
	France	120
	Germany	120
	Portugal	121
	Spain	121
	Sweden	122
	Finland	123
	Norway	124
	Bulgaria	124
	Ukraine	125
	Russia	125
	Georgia	126
	United Kingdom and Ireland	127
	United States	129
	Canada	131
	Chile	132
	Australia	133
	New Zealand	133
	Japan	134
	Iran	135
	Pakistan	135
	Egypt	136

6 Your PhD defence — 142
The big day — 142
- Introduction — 142
- The last days before the defence — 143
- The day of the defence — 145
- Special needs — 146
- Some advice for the defence day from former students — 147
- Some advice for the defence from committee members — 147
- Research insights — 148

Dealing with anxiety on the day of the defence — 152
- Understanding your anxiety — 152
- Strategies for dealing with anxiety on the day of the defence — 153
- Advice from former PhD students — 154
- Advice from committee members — 156

How to handle committee questions — 157
- Relation between defence format and questions — 157
- Understanding the role of the committee members — 157
- Surprisingly easy questions — 158
- Not being able to answer questions — 159
- Long and convoluted questions — 161
- Language-related difficulties with questions — 163
- Advice from former PhD students — 165
- Advice from committee members — 165
- Research insights — 167

Possible difficulties during the defence — 168
- Difficulties related to the committee — 169
- Horror stories and urban myths — 169
- Advice from former students on difficulties — 173
- Advice from committee members regarding difficulties — 174

7	**After the PhD defence**	**178**
	Final graduation requirements	178
	Fulfilling graduation requirements	178
	Distributing your dissertation	180
	Practical tips	180
	Celebrating your achievement	181
	Final recommendations	185
	Further reading	188

Index   193

1 Introduction

The PhD defence as the pinnacle of the PhD trajectory

Your PhD trajectory will typically take a minimum of three years and can take as long as ten years. In any case, it is a huge intellectual and organizational endeavor that will occupy you fully for years and will require an immense effort. And yet there is a pinnacle to this journey! What is it exactly? You say: thesis submission?… Ah yes, that too! Indeed, that is a culmination of all your research and writing up. However, your thesis submission is followed by another (real) pinnacle; that is your thesis defence. Your PhD defence is an event where you defend your thesis in front of experts in your research area. You will present your research, show your contribution to your scientific field, demonstrate that you actually can do an independent research study, and show that you have done it by yourself and that you know what you are doing. You will be examined on how well you can present and communicate your work and how deep is your understanding of the subject and of the results you have produced. You will be assessed and evaluated during your PhD defence and you will receive the final judgement at the end of it. You will be pronounced a Doctor of Philosophy (a PhD). This is the moment when one of your life's dreams comes true, the moment of accomplishment and relief.

DOI: 10.4324/9780429347900-1

We hope that this book will help you navigate a path full of uncertainties towards your thesis defence by giving you guidance on how to prepare for it and what to expect, how to plan it and how to succeed. We will show you some differences in how it is done in different universities and countries. A major part of the preparation for your PhD defence will take place close to the time of the event itself, but there are some aspects you need to work on throughout your *whole PhD journey*. For example, you need to develop your presentation and speaking skills: these take years to learn and practice. So do not leave reading this book until just before your defence. Start reading it today and begin preparing yourself for the positive completion of your PhD journey: a well-planned PhD defence that you successfully pass; it will be the pinnacle of your PhD trajectory.

Scope

The topic of this book is the PhD defence, sometimes also called the *viva voce* or, in short, *viva*. We will use the term "defence", which is commonly used in the United States and continental Europe, throughout except when we discuss national practices and associated terms (e.g., the *viva* for the United Kingdom (Share, 2016)). The term "defence" may imply that the candidate has to "defend" and "battle for" their main hypothesis (Tinkler & Jackson, 2000). As some institutional guidelines contain references to the role of the examining committee in making the candidate feel at ease and avoiding aggressive questioning styles, this term may not be accurate. However, we have opted to stay with "defence" for the writing of this book, placing a side note here on the possible connotations of the term.

While you may think that a book about the PhD defence is limited in scope to an event of just a few hours at the end of your PhD journey, we wanted to write this book because the PhD defence is the pinnacle of your PhD trajectory, and because of the mystery that surrounds the defence in some universities. Depending on your university, your defence may influence the outcome or grade of your PhD or may simply be a formality. We will discuss the differences between defences in various countries in Chapters 2 and 5. Regardless of the official weight associated with the defence, it is an event with a significant emotional value for you as a PhD candidate: it is your moment to celebrate with friends, colleagues, and family. Even when the defence is simply a formality, the emotional stakes are always high.

This book addresses planning and preparing for your doctoral defence and briefly touches upon the topic of what to do afterwards. Most of the activities we describe will take place in the last year of your doctoral journey. In terms of planning, we discuss how you can plan for your defence and set yourself up for success. In terms of preparing for the defence, we discuss practical steps, such as selecting your committee, making your presentation, and preparing for committee questions, as well as preparing mentally for your defence. On the topic of the defence itself, we discuss a wide array of subject matter: from the logistics of the day of your defence, to dealing with spur-of-the-moment anxiety, to addressing unexpected committee questions and difficulties, and how to own the day of your defence. We have included advice from former PhD candidates and committee members. Finally, the last topic in this book is what to do after the defence: how to deal with corrections, how to finalize your graduation requirements, and what to do to mark the end of your PhD trajectory.

If you are a PhD candidate, you may also find this book valuable in other situations during your PhD journey where you have to present and argue in favor of your (proposed) research. Examples of such occasions are the Go/No Go Meeting after the first year of PhD studies in the Netherlands, the Confirmation of Candidature in the first 6 or 12 months in Australia, and the presentation of the proposal in North America. This book could also be insightful for PhD candidates and supervisors in Australia, where an oral defence may not be common: we have included information on the written defence in Australia, and for those Australian universities that are moving towards an oral defence, the testimonies and literature insights in this book can help develop best practices.

We wrote the book for an international audience and find that this approach sets it apart in the literature on the PhD defence. Both within existing textbooks or advice books for PhD students, as well as in the scientific literature on the topic of the PhD defence (see Chapter 2 for our extensive review), most authors consider and investigate only the national context of the PhD defence. However, we wanted to write a book that is useful for students and supervisors worldwide. We included several topics that allow us to have an international outlook: the different formats of the PhD defence (Chapter 2), and a description of the defence in different countries (Chapter 5, based on my (Eva's) PhD Talk blog series "PhD Defences around the world"). This international approach can be particularly valuable if you are defending your PhD in a country that is not where you did your previous studies, or if you are a supervisor who will participate in a committee abroad. This book is suitable for students, supervisors, and committee members in all research fields.

Chapter structures

In writing the book we've brought together various sources: our own experiences as doctoral students, our later-career professional experiences, the literature on the topic of the defence, as well as testimonies from former PhD candidates and committee members from the "Defences around the world" series. You will find that, in referring to our own stories we use the first person, that we refer to testimonies using the citation of the relevant blog post, and that we refer to the literature by citing the reference. In the longer chapters, we've used subchapters to identify and bring together insights from these different sources. In the shorter chapters, we used paragraphs to group the insights. We've followed this sequence: general overview, then former student experiences, then committee member experiences, and then (where relevant) a deeper dive into research insights.

How to use this book as a PhD student

If you are a PhD student, consider this book as a toolkit. We have included information that is useful for PhD students all over the world. Not everything included may be of direct practical value for you: pick the tools you need for your particular situation.

We invite you to read this book from cover to cover first, so that you have a better understanding of the PhD defence and its international context and can assemble your toolkit. Highlight passages that are of particular interest to you, and put placeholders on the pages that contain the most practical information for you. Look out for possible pitfalls ahead. If you are aware of those potential difficulties, you can make life easier for yourself as you sail through them.

As with every book that contains advice, you need to put that advice into practice if you want to reap the benefits of the book. Consider the book your pocket-sized mentor. If you find it useful, set aside time for "meetings with your coach", during which you can actively work on the topics in its pages. For example: reread and reflect on the subchapter on "making your presentation" when you start working on the presentation for your defence.

The caveat with advice books is that it may sound as if there is a single solution that works for everybody. We disagree with this idea: we understand that each thesis, each PhD trajectory, and each PhD candidate are unique (Kamler & Thomson, 2008). From that perspective, our toolbox-based approach aims at serving a wide range of PhD candidates. But, for this approach to work for you, you need to do the work of self-reflection. We are not offering a step-by-step guide to success. Instead, we are presenting food for thought. While this process requires extra effort from you, we are convinced that a deeper understanding of your situation will make you a better researcher.

How to use this book as a supervisor

As a supervisor, you can use this book for two purposes: to help your students plan and prepare for their defence (i.e., as a supervisor for your student) and to prepare yourself to be a committee member abroad (i.e., as an examiner of another student). If you help your students plan and prepare for their defence, you may go through the following steps:

1. Ask your student(s) to read the book to understand the expectations around the defence and associated research findings.
2. Ask your student(s) to revise the chapter on planning towards the defence and prepare a planning for the final year (or other relevant time period) before the defence.
3. Meet each student individually to discuss this planning and expectations, and agree upon a planning and dates for the different milestones towards the defence.
4. Ask your student(s) to revise Chapters 4 and 6, and to list their main contributions as well as list possible committee members.
5. Meet each student individually to decide on the committee (if your institution requires you to select committee members at this point) and discuss the main strengths and weaknesses of the thesis.
6. Ask your student(s) to make a list of possible questions, make a draft presentation, and check institutional requirements.
7. Meet each student individually to go through the possible questions, linking them back to the main strengths and weaknesses of the thesis. Discuss any doubts they may have regarding the procedures, as well as any general concerns regarding questions, committee members, or other worries your student may have.
8. Organize a mock defence or (at least) a rehearsal presentation for your student. Ask faculty members and other PhD students to be present and ask questions, and give feedback.

9 Enjoy your student's defence!
10 Meet after the defence to see how you should implement committee feedback (if the defence is not the final graduation requirement) and to evaluate the defence.

If you use this book to prepare yourself as a committee member for a defence in a different country, you should read it cover to cover. By reading it through first, you will get an unbiased overview of the universal similarities between defences and the expectations and goals associated with these similarities, as well as a deeper insight into international practices. Then, shortly before the defence and after going through the thesis, you can revisit relevant sections. After this quick recap, you can adjust the type of questions you will ask. For example, if you are to serve as external examiner for a *viva* in the United Kingdom, you will be able to ask a large number of questions ranging from philosophical aspects to more detailed questions related to each chapter. On the other hand, if you serve as one of eight committee members in the Netherlands, you may need to prepare a maximum of three questions of a more general nature, each of them sufficiently challenging to serve as your (possibly) only question during the defence.

How to use this book in a classroom setting

Instructors of doctoral training programs can refer to this book in different ways as:

1   background to a module related to preparing for the doctoral defence within a larger doctoral course,

2 course text for a short course on preparing for the doctoral defence, and
3 referenced background reading for a training course for supervisors.

For the first application, we recommend that you schedule half a day to work with students who are one to two months away from their defence. The contents of this module should relate solely to preparing for the doctoral defence. You can assign the following homework:

- Read through this book to gain a thorough understanding of the purpose of the doctoral defence,
- Learn the university regulations regarding the defence,
- List the main strengths, weaknesses and original contributions of their thesis.

During the half day session, include the following:

- Discuss the main findings regarding similarities and differences between doctoral defence formats. Ask students which advice they found particularly helpful, and why.
- Revision of doctoral regulations to see if everyone understands the requirements correctly.
- Discuss emotional aspects related to the defence. Include exercises to teach students how to face anxiety before or during the defence. Exercises may include developing confidence when presenting, the student as the authority on their own research, how to answer unexpected questions, etc.
- Brainstorm possible committee questions. Ask each student to relate possible questions to the strengths and weaknesses of their dissertation.

- Discuss best practices for the presentation.
- Develop a rough plan for the next month(s) or refine the existing plan, and make a checklist for the defence day itself.

For the second application, i.e., a short course for PhD students on preparing for their doctoral defence, we recommend a number of sessions in the final year of the PhD. Table 1.1 gives a possible plan. The first module deals with planning towards the defence with, as its outcome, a draft plan for the final year aimed to submit and defend within the agreed timeframe. The second module deals with the goals of the doctoral defence. Review and discuss the literature related to the doctoral defence and differences and similarities between various defence formats, as well as the university doctoral regulations regarding the defence. The outcome should be that each student understands the university's regulations for the defence. The third module deals with preparing for the defence in a general way: the committee, identifying strengths and weaknesses within your dissertation, preparing for questions, and the emotional aspect of the defence. The fourth module also deals with preparing for the defence but in a more practical way: the presentation (ideally discussing the slides of presentations the students have already prepared), brainstorming possible questions, and practical exercises on how to deal with anxiety before and during the defence. The fifth and final module should take place after the defence and serves as a moment for reflection and evaluation of the defence, the course, and lessons learnt along the way.

For the third application, i.e., as a module within a training course for supervisors, we recommend a half or

Table 1.1 Proposed timeline for series of meetings based on this book to prepare final year PhD students for the defence

Nr	Topic	Duration	Chapters	When?
1	Planning your final year	3 hours	3	1 year before the defence
2	The goal of the defence	2 hours	1, 2	6 months before the defence
3	Preparing for the defence (1)	2 hours	4	2 months before the defence
4	Preparing for the defence (2)	4 hours	5, 6	2 weeks before the defence
5	Evaluation and reflection	2 hours	7	within 1 month after the defence

full day session, during which the following topics can be addressed:

- Discussing the main findings regarding similarities and differences between defence formats. Ask supervisors which preconceived ideas they had about the defence based on their own experience or expectations that, in the light of research findings reported in the book, may have been misguided.
- Brainstorming on best practices for guiding PhD students during their preparations towards the defence, keeping in mind that each student is unique and each may need a different supervision style.
- Revising the university regulations regarding the doctoral defence, see if all supervisors understand the requirements correctly, and discuss any possible misunderstandings or urban legends that may be shared among faculty but are not based on actual regulations.

- Discussing emotional aspects related to the defence. Teach supervisors how to support their students when they are faced with strong emotions, as well as how to explore, understand, and manage their own emotions.
- Discussing how to prepare for serving on committees at universities abroad. Discuss how the findings in the book are in line with or contradict past experiences.
- Discussing how to ask fair and thought-provoking questions during defences and how to prepare students for questions.
- Giving supervisors the tools for setting up a mock defence or departmental presentation.
- Developing self-reflection tools to process insights after each defence in which supervisors have participated.

References

Kamler, B., & Thomson, P. (2008). The failure of dissertation advice books: Toward alternative pedagogies for doctoral writing. *Educational Researcher, 37*(8), 507–514.

Share, M. (2016). The PhD viva: A space for academic development. *International Journal for Academic Development, 21*(3), 178–193.

Tinkler, P., & Jackson, C. (2000). Examining the doctorate: Institutional policy and the PhD examination process in Britain. *Studies in Higher Education, 25*(2), 167–180.

2 Overview of defence formats

History and purpose of the defence

The historical roots of the PhD defence go back to Medieval times. Originally called the 'disputation', the defence (Crossouard, 2011) qualified an individual to become a teacher in the medieval university. The goal of the defence was to show dialectical skills as teaching was based on asking questions. Generation of new knowledge was not required – the Bible was considered the source of all knowledge. Working on dialectical skills was an endeavor for the elite only, as only they could afford to do it. The defence changed with educational reforms in 19th century Germany, where the University of Berlin started to require contributions to research in order to qualify for the doctoral title. This model then spread throughout the world in the 19th and 20th centuries. Research contributions became the standard and the chief criterion for the award of a doctoral degree. The definition of originality related to the PhD has changed over time (Sikes, 2017): *"Up until the end of the 1970s there was an expectation that a thesis should be a scholarly, original life work. From the 1980s onwards it's tended to be seen more as a craft piece*". Nowadays, the PhD defence evaluates whether the candidate has been able to carry out research independently and the focus has shifted from quoting scripture to critical thinking. In addition, the democratization of higher education has made the doctorate accessible to more students, but there are still barriers to entrance for those who have financial dependents. Moreover, new doctoral degrees with different focuses have developed, such as the Doctor of Education (Ed.D, which is the second most popular research doctorate after the Ph.D.) or the Professional Doctorate in Engineering (PD.Eng), which is an industry-oriented degree awarded in the Netherlands (similar to the Eng.D. in the UK).

The defence fulfils different purposes: an oral examination, a celebration, and a rite of passage. Chapter 4 discusses different functions of the defence further and covers how there may be a mismatch between committee members and students in their interpretations thereof. Sometimes, defences are dismissed as meaningless rituals. Compared to other academic ceremonies (Mežek & Swales, 2016) for awarding prizes, honors and degrees, the defence is markedly different in character. It is a high-level discussion between scholars, where you as a candidate will show that you are ready to get your doctoral title and to discuss the independent research you carried out.

The outcome of the PhD defence depends on the defence format. If your thesis is accepted and published before the defence, then it is virtually impossible to fail your defence. If, on the other hand, you defend before you finalize your thesis, the defence may determine the level of revisions needed for the thesis. In many cases (63%, based on a Twitter poll (Lantsoght, 2020)) you will be asked to make minor corrections. While failing your defence is unlikely, it is still possible (5% of respondents), and major corrections are a possible outcome as well (8% of respondents). All in all, 87% of respondents walked out with no or limited work on their thesis after the defence. Similarly, (Ryder, 2014a) found that 84% of candidates in the United Kingdom pass with minor corrections, over 9% with no corrections at all, and fewer than 7% with major corrections. Subdividing these results between Science and Engineering majors and Arts, Social Sciences and Humanities majors showed that the percentage of minor corrections was slightly higher in Science and Engineering where, overall, 93% pass with minor or no corrections. In the Arts, Social Sciences and Humanities the percentage of major corrections is slightly higher.

Defending before or after finalizing the thesis

One of the most important elements of a defence format is the university's requirement for the timing of finalizing and publishing the thesis: before or after the defence. Figure 2.1 shows the steps for both scenarios: defending before the thesis is finalized and defending afterwards. While the overall timeline between draft thesis and graduation may be similar, the point in time when you defend is different.

If you are required to publish the thesis before the defence, then the thesis is a finished product. Your committee will already have approved the thesis for publication and the defence is mostly a formality. A failing grade would be quite shocking. For example, in Sweden (Mežek & Swales, 2016), Belgium (for the second, public, defence), and the Netherlands, the thesis is published several weeks before the defence.

16 Overview of defence formats

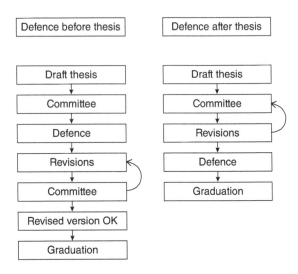

Figure 2.1 Possible defence formats depending on defending before or after finalizing the thesis.

On the other hand, if you are expected to finish your thesis after the defence, you may be less certain about the outcome of the defence. Failing the defence is still highly unlikely since your supervisor would not have allowed you to defend if your work was not worthy of a doctorate. However, since the defence is an integral component of the PhD examination (Remenyi, Money, Price, & Bannister, 2003), it would be technically possible to fail the PhD on the basis of an unsatisfactory oral examination. An analysis of the doctoral regulations from 20 institutions in the UK revealed that in 60% of universities the option of failing the PhD based on an unsatisfactory defence is part of university policy (Jackson & Tinkler, 2001). Most likely, however, you will pass without revisions, with minor revisions, or with major revisions.

Depending on the outcome of the defence and the evaluation of your thesis by the committee, you can expect to spend from a few more days to a few more weeks to finalize your thesis and be cleared for graduation.

Minor corrections are usually the outcome in the USA, so that you can go through commencement as planned, and it is similarly common in Norway and Denmark to make corrections to the thesis after the defence (Anonymous, 2016). In Norway (Kyvik, 2014) the thesis is published before the defence but a resubmission with minor corrections after the defence may be required, whereas in the USA, no form of the thesis will be published before the defence, and the actual submission always takes place after the defence.

Written or oral defence

The most common format of the defence is the oral defence. One common denominator of the oral defence is that the PhD student answers questions – from one or more appointed examiners, or from a committee, and/or from an audience. One of the main challenges with the oral defence is that you need to answer questions on the spot, whereas in the written defence format, you have time to think about any comments. This book mostly addresses the oral defence format and we have therefore included a more extensive discussion on the written defence in this section.

At some universities and in some countries, there is no oral defence and you receive written reports from committee members instead or you work with your committee members until they accept the thesis. The written reports are similar to what you can expect from reviewers after peer review of a journal paper. In the case you work with committee members until they approve the thesis, your committee members will typically be at your university, so that you can meet them frequently while revising your thesis (Berg, 2017).

In South Africa and Australia, the written defence is common because, due to these countries' geographical isolation, flying in experts for the defence from other continents is expensive and time-consuming (Coupland, 2018; Golding, Sharmini, & Lazarovitch, 2014; Remenyi et al., 2003). In Australia, you submit your thesis to the graduate research school. This department then sends the thesis to two (usually anonymous) external reviewers, who review the thesis in the same way research papers are reviewed. After a while, you will receive an email with the outcome of the review process, with possible outcomes from "accept as is" to "significant further work required for thesis to satisfy requirements of PhD". When they require significant further work, you may need to perform extra research or data analysis. After you resubmit the thesis, it goes back to the reviewers. If they then accept it, you can expect an acceptance email. While this system does not include an oral defence, it is great practice for the rebuttal process you go through when working on journal papers. Based on research findings on the written defence format in Australia (Johnston, 1997), we learn that you should see the reviewer as a normal reader (a reader who expects not to get distracted by too many spelling and grammatical errors, and favors a well-written and well-presented document) as well as a scholarly reader (a reader who evaluates your independent research work and favors a thesis that engages with the literature, has a convincing approach and analysis, engages with the findings, and that is publishable). Reviewers evaluate the thesis not only in light of university requirements, but based on their internal assumptions about what makes a doctoral thesis (Holbrook, 2001) and they take their responsibility seriously. A systematic review (Golding et al., 2014) found that reviewers tend to be consistent with each other and are reluctant to fail a thesis.

While the written defence format has been the format of choice in Australia, there is a move towards using videoconferencing tools during the defence (Murugayah, 2019; Regal, 2016; Shields, 2018; Shimabukuro, 2018). Online tools make including committee members from other institutions and regions easier, and reduce travel time and costs, including the associated environmental cost (Spinellis & Louridas, 2013).

Single-step versus two-step defences

While the most common defence format is the use of one defence, some universities use two defences: a private defence and then a public defence. During the private defence, your committee will address all details. You can be alone with only the examiners (as is common at Ghent University (Masuzzo, 2017)), or your committee can include your supervisor and a Chair who is responsible for the formalities (as at Université Catholique de Louvain (Debecker, 2016)). You need to pass the private defence and make amendments to your thesis before you receive approval for the public defence. The public defence is then more of a celebration. In Belgium, the committee dresses in caps and gowns for the public defence, emphasizing the ceremonial part of this event. You can expect more general and broader questions, and sometimes questions from the public, during your public defence.

If you have a single-step defence, then the significance of your performance on the day of the defence depends on when you finalize your thesis, as we discussed in Section "Defending before or after finalizing the thesis". If you defend after your thesis is a finished product, you may have had the in-depth discussions with your committee members in separate meetings. If you defend before your thesis is published, you can expect in-depth feedback during the defence.

At some institutions, the defence itself is broken up into two parts: the defence is public, but with a private part during which the committee asks the candidate more probing questions (Mežek & Swales, 2016). This approach is common in the United States (Lantsoght, 2011). You first have a public part, during which you present your work to friends, family, colleagues, and your committee. The audience can ask questions, and the committee may also ask general questions. After this part, the audience leaves the room and you stay with your committee to answer more in-depth questions. The final part of the defence then consists in the proclamation of the outcome of the defence for the entire audience.

While such two-step defences may not be that common internationally, more and more institutions require PhD students to pass certain milestones during the PhD trajectory. As such, one could argue that there's no such a thing as a single-step defence but that the difference lies in the semantics of what different progress meetings are called. For example, in Chile (Muqoz Llancao, 2016), you have to pass at least two previous evaluations (mini-defences) with the PhD committee before you are allowed to defend your thesis. Within six months, you have to send your thesis to the committee and, if all goes well, you receive the date for a private defence. The public defence is the final step. Similarly, in the United States, most institutions require you to defend your proposal when you are about halfway through your PhD trajectory and in the Netherlands, you may need to pass your Go/No Go meeting after the first year of your PhD studies. This involves defending your proposed approach and planning before a committee.

Public or behind closed doors

We generally tend to think of defences as either public or private. In the strict sense, a private defence is between you and your committee alone and a public defence is open to the public (Abambres, 2019). However, exploring the different formats that are available, we can see that there are different gradations of public and private defences.

While in the strictest sense, the private defence is between you and your committee of examiners alone, there are other formats of private defences where your supervisor and/or a Chair are present. At some universities (Mallinson, 2016), defences are technically public but never advertised, so they become private in practice. Sometimes, the private defence is a step before a more celebratory public defence, as discussed in Section "Single-step versus two-step defences". While the idea is that a private defence allows the committee more critical questions than a public defence, there are no rules set in stone for this – in the end, the way in which committee members examine a doctoral thesis differs between them and between disciplines as individuals have different ideas of what the standard for a PhD should be (Johnston, 1997). Because of this, the way in which the defence is conducted depends on the committee members.

The public defence is a defence your friends, family, and colleagues can attend. However, here again there are differences in format: the questions can come from your committee alone, or from everybody present at the defence.

In Finland (Mikhailova, 2016), it's a formality to ask at the end of the defence if anybody in the audience has any questions but no audience questions are expected. Many public defences have a more celebratory feeling to them, since your friends and family will be there to celebrate with you. While, during a private defence, your committee may examine your thesis on a page-by-page basis, this method is not common for a public defence – it is understood that this approach would bore the audience to death. Therefore, the type of questions you may expect at a public defence can be more general and more related to the core of your argument. But again, it all depends on your committee.

In the light of European standardization of the assessment of PhD theses, there is a debate about the preferable defence format: public or private. A choice on which defence format should be uniform in Europe is not yet made, and the need for such uniformity may not be that urgent given the similarities between defences as we will discuss later in this chapter (see the section "Similarities and differences").

Defence day – fixed schedules and schedules driven by committee

Whether the defence follows a fixed schedule or is driven by the committee depends on the defence format. The difference between a fixed schedule for the defence day and a committee-driven schedule is that you know more about what to expect with a fixed schedule – although the main surprises still lie in the questions you will receive. When you have a committee-driven schedule, you may not know how long the defence will take.

There are different levels of detail in how schedules are fixed as well. For example, in the Netherlands (Muqoz Llancao, 2016), the amount of time the entire committee has for asking questions is pre-determined, the order in which the committee members will ask questions is pre-determined, and the unwritten rule is that the first committee members, who are the external members, will have more time to ask questions. There is however no fixed amount of time for each committee member individually to ask questions in this format.

The total length of the PhD defence (Lantsoght, 2018) is variable. I (Eva) ran a Twitter poll on this topic and half (50%) of the respondents indicated that their PhD defence lasted between one and two hours, with 10% less than one hour, 29% over two hours and 11% in the "other" category. While you may have heard the horror stories of the defences that last for hours on end, such long defences are rather uncommon. The most extreme case that I (Eva) came across in the literature (Remenyi et al., 2003) is an observation that *"there have even been incidents where the viva has run into a second day"*.

Similarities and differences

Similarities

Regardless of the defence format, there are a number of similarities across the different forms of examining. As

Watts (2012) writes: *"Despite its myriad manifestations, the PhD viva voce (live voice), as oral examination of the doctoral thesis, constitutes the final 'test' of the PhD endeavour"*. Golding et al. (2014) argue that the importance of the oral defence is less than that of the thesis. When it comes to written documentation of defence requirements and regulations, Tinkler and Jackson (2000) found that, for universities in the UK, there is a large degree of consistency about "key" criteria. All stated that the candidate should be able to locate their PhD research in the broader context and all but one referred to the candidate displaying knowledge of their thesis. Based on insights from the literature and our own analysis of defence stories, we identify the following similarities among the different oral defence formats:

- Regardless of the format of the defence, you can expect the defence to consist of a *process involving questioning, clarification and discussion of key elements* (Watts, 2012).
- The examiners look for a confirmation that you did the work. If you've had several meetings with your committee members before your defence, or worked with them for parts of your research, then they will already know the answer to this question. If you find your committee members asking a question that seems simple to you during your defence, the goal may be to identify that you did the work.
- The defence tests *"the ability of the student to defend their work, with being 'articulate under stress' seen as an important credential of being a professional researcher"* (Watts, 2012). Even when your defence is a formality, there is the pressure to do well, especially if the event is public.
- The questions depend on your committee members. You can have an idea of what to expect based on

previous meetings and your understanding of their work (and pet peeves), but in the end you can't predict with certainty what to expect.
- You will inevitably go through a number of moments where your work is evaluated prior to the defence. This evaluation can take place in a more formal way, such as during the defence of your proposal, a mini-defence, or a Go/No Go meeting. It can also be less formal, for example: meetings with your committee members, meetings with your supervisor, conference presentations … Every time you show your work to someone else who has the knowledge to provide you with feedback, you put your work out there for scrutiny – which your committee will eventually do in a more official way. Every time you present, you prepare for your defence and learn how to communicate your findings.

Originality

Universities ask for an original contribution as the cornerstone of the PhD. The vague description of originality can create anxiety. So let's look at the literature on this topic first and then let's look at our practical experience with this ill-defined concept. In analyzing the regulations of 20 universities in the UK, the one specification common to all was *"that the candidate's work must provide an original contribution to knowledge to be worthy of the award of PhD"* (Tinkler & Jackson, 2000). According to the official regulations, your defence is the moment to make clear what your novel contribution is – but how is this original contribution defined (Mullins & Kiley, 2002)? It turns out that we can give a variety of definitions to originality, which can be theoretical or methodological, or both (Watts, 2012). In more detail, originality can be one of the following (Golding et al., 2014):

- opening up a new area of research or reframing an old issue;
- introducing a new method, theoretical frame or concept;
- applying established methods, theories and concepts in new areas;
- gathering new data which lead to new findings and conclusions; or
- providing a novel interpretation or synthesis of established data, theories, or conclusions.

Clarke and Lunt (2014) studied the concept of 'originality' in doctoral theses and examination and concluded that:

- doctoral candidates generally have a good understanding of what is expected from them;
- there is a difference between "originality" and "making a contribution";
- the concept of originality **may differ between fields of research**; and
- many examiners also expect the research to be *publishable*.

So, with the definition of originality changing over time and being different in different fields of research, you may ask: "What, after all, is expected from me?" In our opinion, Phillips and Pugh (2010) give the clearest definition (which eschews the use of the word "originality" altogether) of what is expected: the PhD degree is given to you if you can demonstrate that you can carry out research independently.

Differences

While most defences serve the same purpose, the most important differences are:

- The weight of your defence depends on whether or not your thesis is already printed and final before your defence, as discussed in the section "Defending before or after finalizing the thesis". If your thesis is not final before the defence, then your defence may be the moment when your committee changes their recommendation from "minor revisions" to "major revisions", or the other way around. If your thesis is already approved by your committee before the defence and has been printed and distributed, then rest assured: your defence is just a mere formality. Even though you want to do well, you won't win or lose anything by how you perform during your defence.
- If the examination time is limited, the focus of questions may be broader: your research question, your methods and findings, your assumptions, and your work within the larger body of knowledge. If there is no time limit for your defence, and you have not had in-depth discussions with your committee members before it, your committee may go through your thesis on a page-by-page basis.
- One main difference in the defence formats lies in the format of a written defence versus an oral defence. As we've seen in the section "Written or oral defence", a written defence is uncommon internationally and will perhaps even become obsolete as videoconferencing tools improve, but at the moment it is the defence format of preference in Australia and South Africa.

- There is a difference in the function of the defence between the public defence and the private defence, see the section "Public or Behind Closed Doors". A private defence has less of a celebratory function than a public one. When your friends, family, and colleagues all show up for your public defence, the celebratory component is important. Your private defence will still serve as a rite of passage, and you can still celebrate with friends, family and colleagues once you leave the exam room, yet the defence itself will contain fewer celebratory elements.

While there are consistencies in the key *criteria* for the PhD examination, there are significant differences between universities in terms of the *procedures* and *practices* (Tinkler & Jackson, 2000). There is no consensus regarding the role of the defence in the PhD examination process (Jackson & Tinkler, 2001). There's a mismatch in understanding on the role of the defence between examiners and candidates. Academics (142 respondents) identify the purpose of the *viva* as: authentication, examining, monitoring standards, provision of guidance and advice, acting as a rite of passage. Candidates (88 respondents) identified the purpose as: examination and a means to authenticate authorship, but also to harass, humiliate, and make the student suffer. Goulding and Geraghty (2011) carried out a survey of 41 PhD supervisors regarding their preference for PhD defence format. The focus of the survey was on the difference between the British *viva* (behind closed doors, without the supervisor, typically with one external and one internal examiner) and the continental defences (formats vary, but the defences are often public, with a large committee, including the supervisor, examining the candidate) as there is

Table 2.1 Outcomes of survey related to the defence, summarized from Goulding and Geraghty (2011)

Statement	Agree	Disagree	No opinion
Defence in English across Europe	44%	36%	20%
Viva voce examination alone	64%	26%	10%
Panel of examiners and public defence	39%	39%	22%
PhD supervisors should have role in examination	11%	82%	7%
Examiners should include one international member	29%	58%	13%

a push towards unifying defence formats within Europe. The outcomes of the survey related to the defence are summarized in Table 2.1. It is interesting here that UK supervisors prefer to adhere to UK practice (see the level of agreement with statements related to the UK-style *viva* and the level of disagreement with statements related to continental Europe-style defence formats), and do not want general European-level standardization.

Research results on doctoral defence practices and student perception

A number of studies have focused on the perceptions of PhD students about the doctoral defence. Positive perceptions are (Davis & Engward, 2018): being able to present and defend the thesis, and the effort the committee takes in reading and being genuinely interest in the work. Negative perceptions during the defence are (Davis & Engward, 2018): examiners dominating the defence, not having enough opportunities to defend the thesis, unethical practices (being forced to cite the committee member's work), the defence not being fair, and the start of the glass ceiling for female academics (Gallego-Morón, 2017). Candidates have also felt humiliated and alienated when they had to accommodate the priorities of the committee members.

International students, female candidates, students from minority groups, students with disabilities and first-generation academics face additional barriers (Lantsoght, 2021). Respondents from a working-class background have reported that, during their defence, they were reminded of previous assessments not going well and felt more aware of their social class (Crossouard, 2011). Crossouard (2011) found that when the candidate speaks in a "soft" and "searching" way (based on gender or cultural background), the committee may consider the candidate insecure and incompetent. This cultural aspect of the defence is important and is only touched upon briefly in the current literature.

Research has also focused on the emotional aspect of the defence (Davis & Engward, 2018). Even people who describe themselves as calm experience stress and anxiety in the anticipation of the defence, or as a result of the behavior of the committee members. Being prepared helps to manage emotions: practical matters such as timing and layout, coming up with possible questions and answering them in advance, having a mock defence, and being prepared to act "tough".

In terms of practical accommodations, Davis and Engward (2018) found that it is preferable to have the defence in a room with windows, to allow the candidate to be seated closer to the exit, and to provide water.

The majority of students feel well-prepared for the defence and are satisfied with it (Share, 2016). Their reported sources of preparation are as follows: supervisor advice (73%), presentations at conferences (71%), presentation at internal seminars (53%), reading PhD advice books (47%), mock defences (25%), family advice (10%), and *viva* workshops (7%).

Since so many factors and players come together during the defence, we need to be alert for situations where one or more of the players does not act professionally. As a supervisor, you should be aware of possible negative perceptions during the defence and of who could amend the situation during the defence or afterwards. As a committee member, you should be well-informed about the practices and expectations of the university. As a PhD student, you should be aware of the different dimensions of the defence where scholarship, emotions, and culture come together.

References

Abambres, M. (2019). *PhD defenses around the world: A defense in Portugal*. https://www.evalantsoght.com/2019/03/phd-defenses-around-the-world-a-defense-in-portugal.html.

Anonymous. (2016). *PhD defenses around the world: A defense in Sweden*. https://www.evalantsoght.com/2016/04/phd-defenses-around-the-world-a-defense-in-sweden.html.

Berg, M. (2017). *PhD defense around the world: A defense (without a defense) in biology from UC Berkeley*. https://www.evalantsoght.com/2017/10/phd-defenses-around-the-world-a-defense-without-a-defense-in-biology-from-uc-berkeley.html.

Clarke, G., & Lunt, I. (2014). The concept of 'originality' in the Ph.D.: How is it interpreted by examiners? *Assessment & Evaluation in Higher Education, 39*(7), 803–820.

Coupland, K. (2018). *PhD defenses around the world: A defense in neuroscience from Australia*. https://www.evalantsoght.com/2018/02/phd-defenses-around-the-world-a-defense-in-neuroscience-from-australia.html

Crossouard, B. (2011). The doctoral viva voce as a cultural practice: The gendered production of academic subjects. *Gender and Education, 23*(3), 313–329.

Davis, G., & Engward, H. (2018). In defence of the viva voce: 18 candidates' voices. *Nurse Education Today, 65*, 30–35.

Debecker, D. (2016). *PhD defenses around the world: A defense in Belgium*. https://www.evalantsoght.com/2016/05/phd-defenses-around-the-world-a-defense-in-belgium.html

Gallego-Morón, N. (2017). Breaking the glass ceiling – The doctoral thesis defence as a key turning point. *Métode Science Studies Journal, 7*, 113–119.

Golding, C., Sharmini, S., & Lazarovitch, A. (2014). What examiners do: What thesis students should know. *Assessment & Evaluation in Higher Education, 39*(5), 563–576.

Goulding, N. J., & Geraghty, A. (2011). Standards for PhD education in pharmacology in the UK. *Turkish Journal of Biochemistry, 36*(1), 19–25.

Holbrook, A. (2001). PhD examination – assessment's least mapped frontier. *AARE Conference*, Fremantle.

Jackson, C., & Tinkler, P. (2001). Back to basics: A consideration of the purposes of the PhD viva. *Assessment & Evaluation in Higher Education, 26*(4), 355–366.

Johnston, S. (1997). Examining the examiners: An analysis of examiners' reports on doctoral theses. *Studies in Higher Education, 22*(3), 333–347.

Kyvik, S. (2014). Assessment procedures of Norwegian PhD theses as viewed by examiners from the USA, the UK and Sweden. *Assessment & Evaluation in Higher Education, 39*(2), 140–153.

Lantsoght, E. (2011). *A PhD defense at Georgia Tech*. https://www.evalantsoght.com/2011/08/a-phd-defense-at-georgia-tech.html

Lantsoght, E. (2018). *How long does a PhD defense last?* https://www.evalantsoght.com/2018/06/how-long-does-a-phd-defense-last.html

Lantsoght, Eva O.L. (2021) "Students' perceptions of doctoral defense in relation to sociodemographic characteristics." *Education Sciences, 11*(9): 463. https://doi.org/10.3390/educsci11090463

Mallinson, D. J. (2016). *PhD defenses around the world: A defense in political science from Penn State*. https://www.evalantsoght.com/2016/06/phd-defenses-around-the-world-a-defense-in-political-science-from-penn-state.html

Masuzzo, P. (2017). *PhD defenses around the world: A defense in Bioinformatics in Belgium*. https://www.evalantsoght.com/2017/06/phd-defenses-around-the-world-a-defense-in-bioinformatics-in-belgium.html

Overview of defence formats 33

Mežek, Š., & Swales, J. M. (2016). PhD defences and vivas. In K. Hyland & P. Shaw (Eds.), *The Routledge handbook of English for academic purposes* (pp. 361–375). London: Routledge.

Mikhailova, A. (2016). *PhD defenses around the world: A defense in Finland*. https://www.evalantsoght.com/2016/06/phd-defenses-around-the-world-a-defense-in-finland.html

Mullins, G., & Kiley, M. (2002). 'It's a PhD, not a Nobel Prize': How experienced examiners assess research theses. *Studies in Higher Education, 27*(4), 369–386.

Muqoz Llancao, P. (2016). *PhD defenses around the world: Universidad de Chile and University of Groningen, the Netherlands*. https://www.evalantsoght.com/2016/03/phd-defenses-around-the-world-universidad-de-chile-and-university-of-groningen-the-netherlands.html

Murugayah, S. A. (2019). *PhD defenses around the world: A PhD defense from New Zealand*. https://www.evalantsoght.com/2019/05/phd-defenses-around-the-world-a-phd-defense-from-new-zealand.html

Phillips, E., & Pugh, D. S. (2010). *How to get a PhD a handbook for students and their supervisors* (xvi, 258p.). Maidenhead: Open University Press: 1 online resource.

Regal, B. (2016). *PhD defenses around the world: A defense in Modern History and Literature from the USA*. https://www.evalantsoght.com/2016/12/phd-defenses-around-the-world-a-defense-in-modern-history-and-literature-from-the-usa.html

Remenyi, D., Money, A., Price, D., & Bannister, F. (2003). The doctoral viva: A great educational experience of a gun fight at the OK corral? *Irish Journal of Management, 24*(2), 105–116.

Ryder, N. (2014a). *Viva experience research, Part 2: Some statistics*. http://www.nathanryder.co.uk/2014/10/viva-research-part-2/.

Ryder, N. (2014b). *Viva experience research, Part 3: Forming an outline*. http://www.nathanryder.co.uk/2014/10/viva-research-part-3/.

Share, M. (2016). The PhD viva: A space for academic development. *International Journal for Academic Development, 21*(3), 178–193.

Shields, P. (2018). *PhD defenses around the world: A defense from the University of Charleston*. https://www.evalantsoght.com/2018/08/phd-defenses-around-the-world-a-defense-from-the-university-of-charleston.html

Shimabukuro, K. (2018). *PhD defenses around the world: A defense from Literature at the University of New Mexico*. https://www.evalantsoght.com/2018/02/phd-defenses-around-the-world-a-defense-from-literature-at-the-university-of-new-mexico.html

Sikes, P. (2017). And then he threatened to kill himself: Nightmare viva stories as opportunities for learning. *Qualitative Research Journal, 17*(4), 230–242.

Spinellis, D., & Louridas, P. (2013). The carbon footprint of conference papers. *PLoS One, 8*(6), e66508.

Tinkler, P., & Jackson, C. (2000). Examining the doctorate: Institutional policy and the PhD examination process in Britain. *Studies in Higher Education, 25*(2), 167–180.

Watts, J. H. (2012). Preparing doctoral candidates for the viva: Issues for students and supervisors. *Journal of Further and Higher Education, 36*(3), 371–381.

3 Planning for a successful defence

Overall planning of your PhD and possible pitfalls

The duration of a PhD program

It can take from three to ten years to do a PhD, with 32.4% students taking between four and five years, 8.1% less than three years, 27.9% three to four years, and 31.5% more than five years (Lantsoght, 2020c). If you do your PhD studies full-time, it usually takes three to six years to complete a PhD program; sometimes it can take as long as seven years. If you do it part-time, then anything from five to ten years is possible.

The total number of years will depend on the country where you are doing your PhD, as well as the local traditions of your university or the approach of your supervisor.

In the UK it is common to complete a PhD study within 3-3.5 years. PhD funding is often given for this length of study and there are requirements for yearly reports to be submitted to the grad office by the end of each year.

DOI: 10.4324/9780429347900-3

A yearly report is followed by a yearly oral exam in the presence of two internal examiners, or sometimes even in the presence of a larger committee of senior researchers from your university.

You might not appreciate this strict schedule of yearly reports especially if you are behind on the data analysis and interpretation. However, these "hurdles" are helpful in moving you along the process of your PhD, keeping you on track and making you finish on time within the set 3-3.5 years. Also, writing a 25-page report at the end of each year of your PhD might seem like a nuisance, but when you sit down to write your PhD thesis you are likely to be grateful for what you have written earlier in those reports: you are not starting from scratch but have pages and pages of relevant material.

In Germany, the situation is different and it is common to spend more time on a PhD study. You are usually hired by your research institution or the university to work on research projects and these can extend for years and years, thus extending the duration of your PhD. Also, a larger educational load on PhD students, for example in having to complete certain university courses as a requirement of their PhD studies as well as provide a large amount of teaching, contributes to the longer time that students commonly spend on their studies in Germany. It can take five or six years to finally complete your PhD. While your supervisor might be happy for you to just continue working on the projects for longer, you might want to disentangle yourself at some point from this seemingly comfortable position, to finally write up your PhD and move on.

In the Netherlands, a PhD officially takes four years but extensions are possible and commonplace. In fact, only 15% of PhD students graduate within four years

(Belleman, 2015). Just like in Germany, it is common for a PhD student (traditionally called the AIO – Assistant in Training) to work for many years as a research and teaching assistant to the supervisor, and a salaried employee of the university.

In the USA, the median time from the start of the doctoral program to completion was 5.8 years in 2018 (7.3 years from the start of graduate school (NSF, 2019)). These data contradict the common expectation in the USA that a PhD takes three to four years. Typically, the first two years of the PhD are spent on course work where you go to lectures, learn new material, and sit exams. After that you start working on your PhD project, often in tandem with your work doing lab assistant duties (in STEM fields) as well as a lot of teaching (if you are on a Teaching Assistant contract). When you have spent several years in one particular lab, you become an irreplaceable lab assistant who knows everything about the lab and can introduce any new Masters, PhD student or even postdoc to the equipment. So, at some point, you might find yourself in a situation in which it is exceedingly difficult for you to complete your PhD, write it up and move on.

If you do your PhD part-time, that commonly means 50% of the time, and that means it will take you twice as long as a full-time PhD student. About 20% of all PhD students are working on their PhD part-time (with roughly similar numbers for more than, equal to, and less than half-time) (Lantsoght, 2020b), and in my (Eva's) research group, I'm seeing the number of part-time PhD students increase. Spending six to ten years doing it part-time would be considered normal, although in my (Eva's) research group the expectation is that a part-time PhD student finishes in five years. If you have chosen to do your PhD part-time, it probably means you have other commitments and obligations that you spend your time on: this might be because you are a parent (like about 25% of all PhD students (Lantsoght, 2020a)), or because you also have a part-time job, or both: you are a parent and you have a part-time job. It might be that you have a commitment to look after a sick relative or some other call on your time. If you find that other commitments take time during the day, to keep progressing with your PhD studies, you might need to explore working a split-shift at night or in the early morning. While it may be difficult to focus on your work with other commitments and obligations taking priority, knowing exactly what needs to be done based on your planning can help you be productive in short chunks of time (Lantsoght, 2019a).

Juggling so many things and remaining productive in your PhD studies as a part-time student is a big challenge (Jacobs & Winslow, 2004) and planning and discipline are even more crucial than in the case of a full-time PhD student. Factor in the bad reputation of academia for overwork (Lantsoght, 2014, 2019b) and you may feel overwhelmed at the prospect of finishing your PhD. We're here to tell you that good planning goes a long way.

If the PhD project takes much longer than planned there is a risk that the research becomes outdated, especially in a fast-paced field of research. If you are in this situation, you may want to propose a thesis-by-publication to your supervisor: you publish each paper when the research is finished but take the necessary time with your part-time studies to bring all your insights together in the final thesis (introduction + papers + global reflection). With this approach, you get your research out in time within your fast-paced field but manage to balance research and your other responsibilities during the years it takes to complete your entire research project. If you are writing your PhD as a thesis and your research is suddenly published by another research group and/or becomes outdated, you might feel discouraged, but it is still possible to write up your thesis and defend it. Doing it as a formality can be a good strategy here.

Funding and the duration of your PhD

No matter in what country you choose to do your PhD and whether it is full-time or part-time, check the duration of your PhD **funding**! Check how long you have got your scholarship, in other words how long does your PhD funding last? Also check if there are any other extra charges such as, for example, the overseas students fee in the UK, which is quite a large sum of money. Beware of a possible situation that can surface towards the end of your PhD: that you are stuck without funding and still need to do more research, data analysis and writing.

In the Netherlands, the four typical solutions when your funding runs out are as follows:

1 If you are from outside the EU, you will need to secure an income so that your visa can be extended – otherwise you will need to return to your home country and finish writing up there.
2 Most commonly, PhD students being paid for hours spent on a different funded project – but this also means starting to work on a different topic or different experiments from those that will go into your PhD thesis.
3 Another option is to apply for unemployment benefits to support you through the final stages of the PhD – but this route comes with the shame and stigma

associated with unemployment. This option also depends on your visa status, previous work history, and conditions of your PhD contract, so not all PhD students qualify to apply for this support.
4. Finally, you can start working in the industry in a part-time or full-time job and finish your PhD during your early mornings, evenings and weekends.

Beware of getting stuck in a situation where you do not have any money but still need to finish your PhD. What are you going to do if the PhD takes longer and your funding runs out? Think about applying for additional funding close to the time when your funding finishes, saving during your PhD studies, or getting a part-time job and learning to juggle job and PhD (this would however depend on your visa status and whether your PhD contract covers social security). Registering as unemployed and claiming unemployment benefits is a desperate but a valid option. Most importantly, know that you do not have to do it "for free", that you do have living expenses, and that they can possibly be covered by a new pot of money or additional scholarship. You need to get enough confidence to ask your supervisor or your department for additional help, or look for additional funding elsewhere. If you are a foreign student and the end date on your work permit and visa is drawing near, let your supervisor know that you will need to find a solution or leave the country. Do not just continue hiding your situation and suffering in silence and isolation. Reach out for help.

Sources of delays during the PhD

Certain circumstances in your research and in your personal life can alter your planning, affect your progress,

Planning for a successful defence 41

and cause your PhD studies to stretch out for many more months or even years. Difficulties in your research can seriously affect your planning and delay your progress. Such difficulties could be an experimental set-up that is not working or a piece of equipment that breaks down so that you are unable to collect your data. It might be that the data analysis is much more complex than anticipated, or that the research direction you have chosen was a dead end and you need to start from scratch after spending months working hard in this particular direction. If you are developing an experimental method, building a new set-up from scratch, and it keeps malfunctioning, then it could sabotage the success of your whole PhD. Without collecting data on this new setup, you have no data to analyze, and nothing to write about in your PhD thesis. If you are lucky, your supervisor will spot the problem and help you change direction or focus on something new. However, if that is not the case, it is your responsibility to reassess the progress of your PhD and decide to start something new before it is too late. Have a plan B for the worst-case scenario.

There may be a problem with the visa for the country in which you are doing your PhD, and that could force you to go to your home country and spend considerable time away from the university of your PhD studies. This will result in losing some of your precious PhD time. Make sure you check your student visa duration and plan accordingly.

Difficulties in a relationship with a supervisor or a colleague in the lab can severely affect the progress of your PhD, and even stall it for months that can turn into years. A complete breakdown in communication with the supervisor because of disagreements is rare but not non-existent. A supervisor bullying the PhD student also occurs (e.g. verbal abuse, non-constructive criticism, openly or subversively telling the PhD student they are not good enough or their work is not good enough, or throwing tantrums in front of them), and this can turn your PhD experience into hell and delay completion significantly. Along the same lines, a PhD supervisor can lose interest in a project when they see that it may not lead to high-impact publications, or because a new topic has grabbed their attention, or because they have advanced in their career and taken up a leadership or more administrative role within the university, or are taking an important service appointment. Your supervisor may also make a career move to another university and your supervision relationship may change as a result.

Personal circumstances, sometimes unexpected, can alter your planning and add years to the time you spend on your PhD studies. Ill health, in particular a chronical illness, can take months or even years out of your study. This is a valid reason to take some time off from your PhD studies. Make sure to inquire at your University whether you can have an official break (which will temporarily stop the clock on your PhD studies) and whether you can apply for an extension for this reason. The birth of a baby, unexpected injury, or illness of a relative are other examples of personal circumstances that can affect the planning and duration of your PhD studies. It is important to stay in communication with your supervisor and the grad office about it, officially arrange a break in your PhD studies, and apply for an extension if this is what is needed.

In today's digital age, distractions and disruptors to our attention are everywhere and many PhD candidates report finding it difficult to stay focused, which can then lead to slowing down your overall progress. I (Eva) struggled with this during my PhD, and that was before the arrival of the smartphone. My best advice to deal with these digital distractions is to switch off your phone, close your internet browser, disable your WiFi – whatever is necessary to stay away from the distraction. Work on a specific, small, and achievable task for a short amount of time. Take frequent breaks away from your work and your screens – for me, drinking a cup of coffee outside or going for a walk are breaks that work very well. Check out the resource for dealing with digital distractions on Olga's website (Degtyareva, 2021a). Besides removing the temptation of distractions, it's also valuable to try and understand the reasons why you are pulled towards these distractors. Are you bored or unmotivated? Are you afraid of not doing the task well? Is your head too busy? Going through this inner work is a key to understand the deeper reason for your struggles.

Changes and restrictions of a more global nature can also intervene with your PhD plan. It might be a natural disaster such as an earthquake or a storm that affects your lab and your research. It might be that there are irregularities with the electricity and water supply in your area because of the political or economic situation. An example of such a situation is the experience of a student working on her MSc in microbiology in Chile when an 8.8 Mw earthquake hit the country. To save their samples, she and her colleagues had to head out to a hardware store to rent a generator to keep the freezers working (Gonzalez-Muñoz, 2017).

As we write this chapter in April 2020, the whole world is affected by an unprecedented change. In a lot of countries people are directed by their governments to stay at home, our university departments and research labs are closed, and our kids are at home too as the schools are closed. These are the measures to contain a coronavirus that spread throughout the world in January-March 2020. As the result of these measures, scientific meetings and research conferences are cancelled, visits to other labs are cancelled, travel to central facilities to collect data is cancelled, field work is cancelled, in-person interviews you planned for your studies are cancelled, and in-person meetings with your supervisor are cancelled. PhD defences are also cancelled or moved to an online setting.

You may have been advised to leave your place of study and travel back to your home country. Your on-campus housing arrangements may not be available to you anymore. So you might find yourself stuck in your parents' house in the small room where you grew up, not able to do any of your experiments, field work, interviews or simulations, and unable to see your supervisor or your peers in person. You might feel lonely and isolated, full of worries about news of the rising death toll due to the virus around the world, finding it hard to focus on your writing because of anxiety, and not even be able to go outside for some fresh air or exercise. It might be tough to be all the time in the house with your parents, or to share your home office with your spouse. If you have kids, you suddenly find yourself spending most of your time homeschooling, childminding, and entertaining them (Lantsoght et al., 2021). And if you have small kids, that is one of the toughest situations to be in –with little ones trapped inside a house or a flat chaos prevails, and nothing gets done.

All in all, this might be the biggest change of plans **yet**! As we are writing this section, we don't know how long this situation will last, how universities will officially respond to the delays that occur, and what the world will look like when the restrictions are removed. Will the number of available flights be much lower as airlines go bankrupt? Will we be able to travel to conferences, places of fieldwork etc. again in the future? Will more conferences go fully online, as organizers notice that this method can include a more diverse group of scholars? How will the recession affect all of us? Right now, it is important that you discuss all the areas of your work affected by this situation with your supervisor. Discuss what you can do and what you can't do. If, technically, you could work (i.e. you have your data, all your software is up and running) but you find yourself consumed by anxiety because of this situation – don't hide this difficulty from your supervisor.

Hard deadlines for the PhD duration

Some universities have a requirement for a PhD study not to exceed a certain number of years. Check for any such requirements at your university that would put a cut-off date on the submission of your thesis. For example, some universities might have a requirement of seven years for the submission of a thesis and if you don't submit your thesis within that time, you are simply removed from the PhD program and from the department, with no further extension or negotiation possible. Another possible hard deadline may be the time your supervisor can graduate you after their retirement. My (Eva's) promotor[1] retired in 2012, and all his PhD students had to graduate by 2017 – five years after retirement is the maximum time for having the right to promote a student in the Netherlands.

If you have any prolonged health issues or you are having a baby, remember to contact the graduate office to enquire if you can officially pause your PhD studies to give yourself time to recover from illness or look after your little one. If you manage to officially pause your PhD clock, you can then un-pause it when you are ready, thus giving yourself more official time to work on your PhD. Overall, it will take longer to complete your PhD, but at least you won't be kicked out of the PhD program while you are sick or looking after your baby. Make sure to ask for legal advice about your rights: if you are a woman in a male-dominated department, supervisors may simply not be aware of how to arrange for such situations (Kachchaf et al., 2015).

One of my (Olga's) clients shared that she had not frozen her PhD when she had her daughter and when working in a company part-time. So, during all that time she was not actually working on her PhD, the PhD clock was still ticking and counting the years. At the end she was running out of time and found it really stressful to write up and submit before the 7-year limit was up.

Planning towards your defence

Now that we have discussed various challenges and pitfalls that can alter your planning and delay the completion of your PhD, let's go back to planning the duration of your studies in an ideal case, as it is a good place to start. The more detailed your plan, the more likely it is that you are going to finish in accordance with your plan. It is common for PhD studies to take a bit longer (or a lot longer) than you plan; you will find yourself revising and extending your own deadlines many times over. And yet this does not devalue the power of planning. You can **view the planning as a catalyst for starting your work, the set plan with deadlines and intermediate milestones will get you in gear and get you moving**.

If things take a bit longer that is ok. After all, you are in unknown territory: you are likely researching something that no one has done before. By the very nature of a PhD study, you are venturing into something that **you have not done before**, so planning can be challenging. At the same time, your planning can help to function as a roadmap for how, globally, you will approach your PhD studies. One of my (Olga's) coaching clients, a PhD student in Singapore, said that she ended up scrapping every timeline, every plan she wrote, as unplanned events always happened and everything took longer than expected. And yet, she has managed to write up and submitted her PhD thesis on the last permitted day of her studies, 31st of December. She has now defended her PhD and moved on in her career and in her life.

So it is very important that you create a plan! Allow it to evolve and change, modify it with time, but continue to stick to it, as it will help you identify the tasks that need to be done and will help you to move along towards your goal.

Let's see what the overall plan for a 3-year full-time PhD study in experimental science can look like:

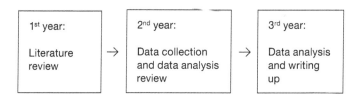

This is an ideal (clean) plan, but in reality, it will probably look more tangled up. You might find yourself doing your literature review in the first year and already starting data collection, especially if your lab already has a streamlined data collection facility. In the second year, you might find yourself doing more data collection and analysis, but also reading more literature for the next stage of the project or for an entirely new project that might form another results chapter in your PhD thesis. In the third year, you might still find yourself doing a lot of data collection and data analysis and you will also be writing up for sure.

If you do your PhD by papers and you are going to submit your PhD thesis as a collection of your papers with a written introduction and conclusions, then plan for your PhD might look as follows. This example is given for a 3.5 years full-time PhD in experimental science:

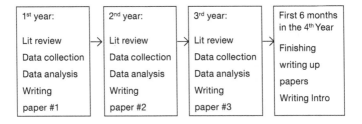

There is a saying among academics: if you write 100 words a day you will never need to write your PhD. So, create an outline of your PhD thesis in the early stages of your PhD and let it guide and motivate you throughout your studies. Get in the habit of writing down a bit every day, filling in the blanks of the outline you have created. "Writing your thesis" does not have to be something you do at the end of your studies. If you are working on your experimental set-up, put a description into writing as soon as possible. This will be the draft of your methods chapter. If you are doing your literature review, don't just read and take notes on bits of paper. Create a file called "literature review" where you can type up your notes and bibliography or develop your database of references in reference management software. If you do not type up your references or store them in reference management software, it might take you ages to do it at the end of your thesis writing, which can be stressful when you run around frantically just before submission of your thesis. You can do many of those things well in advance, in fact years before submission. All these ideas are possible if you work on your PhD with submission in mind.

To write up the thesis bit by bit throughout the whole duration of your studies is indeed a great idea. However, in reality many PhD students leave the writing until the very end.

If you find yourself in a situation when there are only three to six months left until submission and you need to write your entire thesis, it is a good idea to clear your time to **only work on writing up your thesis**. You will need all the time you can get. The enormity of the task can seem daunting and might make you feel overwhelmed, worried, anxious, panicky and frantic. However, with proper planning, discipline, and consistent action, it is possible to write up your thesis in those three to six months (depending on how much is still left to do). To give yourself as much time as possible, you can discuss the situation with your supervisor and agree that you will completely stop doing any more data collection to allow you to focus on writing. It can also help if you stop, reduce, or postpone any other commitments or obligations you might have such as: teaching, grading, attending seminars or conferences, or being part of committees. If you need to write six chapters and have six months left, allocate three weeks per chapter to leave enough time at the end for revision, editing and proofreading.

You can learn more about planning the last year of your PhD in another book in this series (Firth et al., 2021).

It is important to know your options and decide in advance whether you are going to do your PhD by papers or by writing a thesis. Clearly, the focus of your PhD is on producing a good thesis and defending it but, for your subsequent career, having published papers at the end of your PhD gives you a huge advantage. So writing papers for publication throughout your PhD could be a good idea. Of course, check with your university what the rules are around that as, for example, in Germany the work of PhD students has to be published for the first time in their thesis. Some universities have publications built into PhD graduation requirements (for example in some departments in Belgium): you would need to have a certain number of papers submitted to be admitted to the thesis defence.

Writing papers for publication is also a great way to learn to write and it can help you immensely when writing your thesis. It is in a way easier to make a paper into a thesis chapter than a thesis chapter into a paper. And there is the bonus of having a couple of papers on your CV by the end of your PhD studies when you apply for a postdoc or for some other jobs. The drawback is that it may be more difficult to write a PhD by publication in the last months of your funding as your work may be rejected by one journal after which you need to alter it to suit the requirements of a different journal.

For your inspiration, look at several real-life timelines of various PhD students, written down **after** they have received their PhD (Degtyareva, 2021b). These timelines illustrate how much time everything takes, what kind of requirements you need to take into account, and what unexpected situations can influence the course of your PhD. You can use these timelines to help you create your own plan (Degtyareva, 2021b).

Working on your PhD with the defence in mind

From research ideas to research planning

> I don't think I knew anything about planning when I started my PhD. I knew what area I wanted to investigate, and I wrote a proposal for the supervisor, that was **three** PhD studies, not one. Most of the learning happened as I went along.

This is what one of my (Olga's) star clients shared when I asked her how she planned her PhD studies. She has just got her PhD and during her studies she has published several papers which were well received in the research community, while overcoming her own challenges of moving her entire family to a different continent, changing university, and being bed-bound for months due to an accident. She added: *"Everything took longer than I expected – getting approvals, reading, and writing"*.

Another client, from Portugal, who spent seven years part-time on her PhD having worked part-time and given birth to a baby during that time, adds: *"It was more difficult than anticipated, and it all took more time than expected"*.

Many PhD students I have talked to, and I myself (Olga), approached their PhD studies in a similar way: we thought about the research topic and were keen to start with the literature review and data collection but knew little about planning. You might find yourself in a similar position: you might not know much about project management or planning a long extensive project. After all, it is likely that you have never before in your life undertaken such a huge independent piece of work that could take three to ten years of your life and occupy you so fully, that has so little structure, and requires so much of your input, creativity, knowledge, planning, studying and execution.

So it is a good idea, alongside doing your research, that you also learn about planning and project management. You should definitely look out for any workshops on these topics your department or university are running: they are usually well worth attending. And do some reading about this topic. One of the books we strongly recommend is *Seven habits of highly effective people* by Steven Covey (1989). It has been so influential in my (Olga) becoming more productive and successful in my research career. One of the habits is called: "Begin with the end in mind". As the title of this section says: you need to learn to "work on your PhD with the defence in mind". This means that you need to see yourself clearly in your mind defending your PhD and then frequently ask yourself: "What do I need to do today to get myself closer to my goal?" Checking in regularly will help you stay on track.

Planning for different types of PhD programs

Some PhD programs are well-structured, with yearly reports and exams at the end of each year. These requirements are useful in breaking up the long PhD journey into smaller, more manageable periods that create intermediate deadlines and milestones and help you stay accountable and on track. This kind of structure also lets you know that any particular stage of your PhD is going to last for only a finite period of time and that after a certain time you will move on. Regardless of whether you are part of a structured PhD program or not, it is important to develop this kind of mindset for your PhD studies: no stage is going to last forever, and even if it is difficult, it will eventually be over and you will move on to the next stage.

If your PhD program does not have a rigid structure, you and your supervisor may still need to develop deliverables for your funders. If that's the case, make sure to plan around these deliverables and take the opportunity to finish off an important part of your work for each deliverable.

If your PhD program does not have this kind of structure in place however, you will need to create intermediate deadlines and milestones for yourself. If there is no deadline, no work gets done. Parkinson's law states that work expands to fill the time available for its completion. So, if you don't have a deadline, the work will expand and occupy you for as long as you allow it to. You can do a literature review that is infinitely long, digging deeper and deeper into existing literature, and there are still many new papers coming out every day. You can occupy yourself digging deeper and reviewing freshly published papers for months or even years. And yet you will need to put a lid on it and say: "*This is as far and as deep I go*". You will need to outline the boundaries of your literature review and submit it to your supervisor in some form.

In addition, it is all too easy to get off track and get stuck on one particular stage of your studies, especially if it is not working as planned. If you're not progressing at all you will need to decide at some point about how to proceed and move on following a plan B. Also, staying stuck in one particular stage for longer than needed can be a form of procrastination. Sometimes you might justify delaying a start to work on your next chapter by saying you are busy improving and refining your current PhD chapter. Be aware of this dynamic and give yourself set deadlines for wrapping up every stage even when it is not perfect or entirely complete, and for moving on to the next stage. A strategy you can use here is to set daily word count targets, allowing yourself to take time off when you have reached your daily target and motivating yourself on more difficult days to soldier on and meet your goal.

My (Olga's) client from Australia says *"Ability to move on is very important. You can spend too long on one part, and not leave enough time for the rest. So, beware of this, and keep moving"*.

When you plan your research, it is important to know the demands (or lack thereof) in your program, as we've seen for different situations above. A lack of clear milestones can be a major challenge – so define these milestones for yourself, plan with the thesis submission and defence in mind, and reflect on how different tasks will contribute to answering your research question.

Prepare for your defence by giving talks throughout your PhD

At the end of your PhD you will need to present your thesis in one way or another: either by having a PhD defence or by presenting a completion seminar (Berg, 2017). A great way to prepare for it is to practice giving talks and seminars throughout the entire duration of your PhD studies. In a study by Share (2016) (see section "Research results on doctoral defence practices and student perception", 71% of respondents said they prepared for their defence by presenting at conferences and 53% by presenting at internal seminars. Public speaking and answering questions at the end of your presentation are skills that take time to develop, and it is very difficult or even impossible to acquire them at short notice. In particular, if you are scared of public speaking, tend to freeze when presenting in front of other people and don't do well answering an audience's questions, you will need to start practicing sooner rather than later. Include time for conferences in your overall planning: time to write a conference paper and to prepare your presentation. Look for seminars and industry events in which you can participate as a speaker.

In Chapter 4 you will see how to prepare for the examiners' questions and what the examiners look for when assessing your presentation. In the section "How to prepare for committee questions", you will learn that your presentation is likely to be judged on how fluent it is, and how confidently and articulately you present. You will also see that one of the fears that comes up before the thesis defence for many PhD students is freezing when answering questions or being unable to answer questions. The best advice for overcoming this fear is to present a lot and practice going through this situation again and again until you feel more comfortable with presenting and answering questions. The problem with this advice is that it is difficult to master this skill at short notice and it usually requires years of practice: make sure to start early.

At this moment, many face-to-face conferences and events are cancelled because of the COVID-19 pandemic. You may be wondering how you can practice your presentation skills in this situation. Avenues to explore include the possibility of organizing virtual departmental seminars, participating in online conferences, and hosting online coffee breaks with your fellow PhD students to discuss your progress and ask each other critical questions. If such events are currently not happening, you can take the lead to organize them.

So, working on your PhD with the defence in mind also means giving yourself enough opportunities to speak in public: at group and lunch time seminars, industry events and conferences. If you do it several times a year for the few years of your PhD, by the end of your PhD you will be much more skilled in presenting your work and in handling yourself when answering questions after each presentation. You will simply know what to expect and it will not be so scary.

Document your PhD journey

Keeping a research journal or documenting your thought processes throughout the PhD is very valuable. You will not write out all the iterations of a thought that you had in your PhD thesis, but it may be helpful to be able to revisit your thought processes on certain parts of your work when you prepare for the defence.

There are many different ways in which researchers keep a research journal. If you need some help getting started with reflective practice for your research, I (Eva) have a template on my website for those who subscribe to my newsletter. You can practice with such a template for a while before you start developing your own research journal entry. If you do experimental or field work, your lab or field notes can be the right venue for jotting down some ideas on your progress and thought processes. If you are at an earlier stage of your PhD, for example during the literature review, then a designated notebook could serve as your research journal.

I (Eva) used various forms of reflective practice during my PhD: my lab notes, short reports typed out throughout my PhD, my monthly progress monitor in which I included questions for reflection, my personal journal, and handwritten pages with notes that I added to the same folder as my labnotes.

Note

1 Term used in the Netherlands for advisor or supervisor. In order to be able to act as a promotor, he/she needs to have "ius promovendi", the right to promote, the conditions for which are prescribed in Dutch law.

References

Belleman, B. (2015). *Promovendi Haken Massaal Af*. http://delta.tudelft.nl/artikel/promovendi-haken-massaal-af/29784.

Berg, M. (2017). *PhD defense around the world: A defense (without a defense) in biology from UC Berkeley*. https://www.evalantsoght.com/2017/10/phd-defenses-around-the-world-a-defense-without-a-defense-in-biology-from-uc-berkeley.html.

Covey, S. R. (1989). *The seven habits of highly effective people: Restoring the character ethic*. New York: Simon and Schuster.

Degtyareva, O. (2021a). *Distractions*. http://www.olgadegtyareva.com/distractions

Degtyareva, O. (2021b). *Timelines*. http://www.olgadegtyareva.com/timelines

Firth, K., Connell, L., & Freestone, P. (2021). *Your PhD survival guide: Planning, writing, and succeeding in your final year*. Insider Guides to Success in Academia series. Oxon: Routledge.

Gonzalez-Muñoz, B. (2017). *How to work in a microbiology lab after an 8.8 earthquake*. https://www.evalantsoght.com/2017/01/how-to-work-in-a-microbiology-lab-after-an-8-8-earthquake.html

Jacobs, J. A., & Winslow, S. E. (2004). Overworked faculty: Job stresses and family demands. *The Annals of the American Academy of Political and Social Science, 596*(1), 104–129. doi:10.1177/0002716204268185.

58 Planning for a successful defence

Kachchaf, R., A. Hodari, L. Ko, and M. Ong. 2015. Career-Life Balance for Women of Color: Experiences in Science and Engineering Academia. *Journal of Diversity in Higher Education* 8 (3):175–191. doi: 10.1037/a0039068.

Lantsoght, E. (2014). *Workloads in academia*. https://wakelet.com/wake/09427364-1eb1-440a-b576-1edac53998d8.

Lantsoght, E. (2019a). *Tips for working at night*. https://www.evalantsoght.com/2019/05/tips-for-working-at-night.html

Lantsoght, E. (2019b). *Working hours in academia*. https://www.evalantsoght.com/2019/02/working-hours-in-academia.html

Lantsoght, E. (2020a). *Parenting during the PhD*. https://www.evalantsoght.com/2020/04/parenting-during-the-phd.html

Lantsoght, E. (2020b). *Part-time or full-time PhD?* https://www.evalantsoght.com/2020/05/part-time-or-full-time-phd.html

Lantsoght, E. (2020c). *Time to completion of the PhD*. https://www.evalantsoght.com/2020/04/time-to-completion-of-the-phd.html

Lantsoght EOL, Tse Crepaldi Y, Tavares SG, Leemans K and Paig-Tran EWM (2021) Challenges and Opportunities for Academic Parents During COVID-19. *Frontiers in Psychology – Educational Psychology*. 12:645734. doi: 10.3389/fpsyg.2021.645734

NSF. (2019). *Survey of earned doctorates*. https://ncses.nsf.gov/pubs/nsf20301/data-tables/.

Share, M. (2016). The PhD viva: A space for academic development. *International Journal for Academic Development, 21*(3), 178–193. doi: 10.1080/1360144X.2015.1095759.

4 Preparing for your defence

There will be several weeks, if not months, between the submission of your thesis and the day of your defence. In this chapter we discuss what these weeks and months are going to be filled with. You will learn how to make your presentation and how to practice it, how to organize your committee, how to schedule your defence, and how to prepare for the committee questions. We will also talk about how to deal with the anxiety before thesis submission and before the defence. In this chapter, you will find our advice, as well as sections with advice from former PhD candidates, committee members, and insights from the literature, with references that can guide you to deeper reading if you want it.

Preparing for all elements of your defence

Elements of the defence

What your defence looks and feels like depends on the defence format. We have reviewed the different characteristics of the defence in Chapter 2 and in Chapter 5 you will

DOI: 10.4324/9780429347900-4

learn all about the different formats of the defence around the world. Regardless of the defence format, however, the following elements typically make up the defence:

- opening words,
- presentation,
- questions,
- deliberation,
- conferral of outcome of defence, and
- closing words.

The Chair of the defence committee usually gives the opening words. Whether or not there are also ceremonial procedures related to the opening words depends on the defence format. The presentation comes in different forms. In some cases, it is the main committee member who has to present the thesis instead of the student. When you get to present your thesis yourself, you may be asked to prepare a full seminar-length presentation on your research, or you may be asked to briefly summarize what you did, without slides. In some cases, the presentation takes place before the actual defence (and thus before the opening words). In the section "Making your presentation", you will find advice on how to prepare for your presentation.

The main part of the defence is the answering of questions from the committee. We will discuss how to prepare to answer committee questions in the section below. After the Q&A part of the defence, the committee typically withdraws to deliberate on the outcome. When they return, they will tell you the outcome and give their evaluation of your thesis. To finalize procedures, the Chair may add closing words explaining to you what happens next. In some countries, the closing words include the graduation ceremony and the *laudatio*[1] by the promotor.

Preparing to answer questions

While we will come back later to the topic of answering questions, it is important to understand the purpose of the questions from your committee members during the defence. As Brennan (2019) stated: *"Examiners will want to know whether you did the research and wrote the dissertation, whether you understand the research, whether you addressed the research questions and whether they were addressed in a suitable manner".* The first purpose is to verify your authorship. If you did the work and did not cheat and plagiarize, then you don't have to worry about this. The second purpose is to examine your understanding of your work, the research question (which should always be linked to the literature and the broader context of your field of study), and your methods. Your committee members also look into your conclusions and at what your work means in the broader scope of your field.

Practical aspects

Make sure you understand the regulations of your university regarding the defence (Brennan, 2019). What are the possible outcomes of the defence? What is the role of your committee members? What steps do you need to take after the defence?

The next practical aspect you need to understand is what happens on the day of the defence (Brennan, 2019). First of all, make sure you understand all elements from your defence format (revise the different elements in Chapter 2 if necessary).

- Do you need to prepare a presentation? How long should it be?
- How long should you expect the defence to last?

When you understand your defence format, make sure you are clear about who will attend your defence and who can ask questions. Besides knowing what to expect, think about the nitty gritty:

- Where will your defence take place?
- Is the room/hall suitable for your defence?
- What do you need to bring?
- Do you need to coordinate something with the IT department?
- If at least one of your committee members joins through videoconference, what do you need to prepare: the online meeting room, speakers, videoconferencing tools …?

Research insights on preparing for the defence

When it comes to the purpose of the doctoral defence Watts (2012) points out that

> it is not always clear if it is the thesis (as a complete and comprehensive document) or the student (as an apprentice researcher) that is being examined at the *viva*, with some differences discernible across disciplines. With such uncertainty, getting students ready for the *viva* is like preparing in the dark.

The recommendation then is: "*without a standard format to follow and variability in duration, development of effective strategies aimed at a positive outcome requires judicious attention*".

Morley, Leonard, and David (2002, 2003) observe that the defence in the UK is *"ill-defined as to whether it is a one- or two-stage assessment process, and what the relative weight of the thesis is to the viva"*.

According to de-Miguel (2010) (reflecting on the practice in Spain), the defence should serve two purposes:

1 The candidate should be able to communicate the contents of their research work clearly in the appropriate language of the field of study and by using suitable graphic material, and
2 The candidate should be able to argue the research findings, the answers to the research question, and any advance in the area of knowledge.

de-Miguel (2010) proposes to evaluate the defence based on the clarity of the presentation as well as the adequacy of the defence.

In terms of advice and best practices, Watts (2012) cautions that

> As doctoral *viva* examinations have been shown to be so variable in their form and conduct, it is difficult to offer students detailed and comprehensive guidance about how to best prepare. Also, of course, students are highly individual, with each having their preferred ways of approaching the preparation task.

However, she then continues formulating advice on how best to prepare for the defence. The first recommendation is to go back and read the thesis to get back up to speed with its contents. It may be useful to create a road map or overall flowchart of the thesis. Watts (2012) says:

> Detailed familiarization with the thesis may seem a very obvious starting point, but I can recall two occasions when colleagues, in the role of PhD examiners, reported that it was clear that, in the case of both students, they had not read or were not thoroughly familiar with the thesis content. Re-familiarization with the context, research questions, literature, key findings, and the conclusion should, therefore, be a primary aim of the read-through because, without this, candidates are unlikely to be able to offer an adequate defence of their work.

The second read of the thesis can focus on areas of potential debate, particularly where these relate to the literature or methods.

Watts (2012) emphasizes that *"knowing your thesis inside out"* is a vital component of effective preparation. When you read your thesis again, focus on the strengths and weaknesses of your work that may not have been evident when you were writing it up. Be prepared to acknowledge these strengths and weaknesses and to show awareness and critical reflection on your own work in hindsight. When work involves new discovery but there remains uncertainty and no absolute right answer, be clear about issues such as generalizability of findings, limitations of the study and areas for further research. If your work relates to a current controversy or debate, committee members are likely to ask questions that address this issue – you may experience these probing questions as criticism of your work, but they may simply reflect the curiosity of the committee members.

Wellington (2010) studied the pedagogy involved in preparing students for the doctoral defence, and their expectations, in the UK. Students anticipate their defence through a number of lenses: "*a rite of passage, a process of legitimation, a major event for decision making, the end of an era, a stamp of approval, an entry or admittance process, a chance to shine, closure, a climax, and a platform*". To study this further, the author collected data from 16 focus groups, each with 10 to 16 students. In these focus groups, students reflected on four topics:

- their positive feelings and anticipations about the defence,
- their negative feelings and attitudes,
- what they knew about the defence, and
- what they didn't know yet.

When it came to positive anticipations, the author identified eight categories (Wellington 2010):

1 *feelings of the end, the climax, the start of a new life,*
2 *a unique opportunity for feedback, improvement and dialogue with experts,*
3 *an event of legitimation and acceptance,*
4 *an opportunity for clarification, explanation and defence,*
5 *a chance to show emotion and enthusiasm,*
6 *anticipations of utility, formative feedback and future development,*
7 *feelings of confidence,*
8 *a chance to reflect, tell the story, and consolidate.*

The four categories of negative anticipations were:

1 *fears about the outcomes,*
2 *worries about themselves before or during the viva,*
3 *apprehensions relating to the examiners, their questions, and their comments,*
4 *anxieties about post-viva feelings.*

In terms of what the students knew about the defence, many commented that the purpose was to defend their thesis. In addition, students understood the purpose of checking the veracity and authorship of the thesis. In terms of the nature of the examination, some students mistakenly described it as a quiz or a friendly chat, whereas others were aware of its intellectual intensity. There was confusion about the possible outcomes of the defence, the duration of the exam, the rules and regulations for the conduct of the defence, and the appointment and behavior of the committee members. Most students get their information from friends who have already passed their defence. Based on the data analysis, we can learn the following:

> 1) students want to experience a defence "*in which they will be challenged, be asked to articulate their work, to justify and clarify, to tell 'their story' and to engage in deep discussions, with 'experts' in their field*" and
> 2) "*they want it to be a formative process – they want feedback, they want to improve, and they want it to be a platform for further development. They want a 'quality experience' not necessarily an easy ride*".

Another observation from the study is that students need and want preparation for the defence. In addition, the data provide evidence for keeping the defence and improving it.

The defence evaluates three components: skills, content and conduct (Wellington, 2010). Skills can be prepared for to a large extent. For example, *"skills of communication and debate can be 'acquired' by giving students access to 'academic research cultures'"*, which can include "*attendance at conferences, internal and external seminars, and contact with internal and external networks. Thus, they will experience 'ways of speaking' and engaging in different types of 'academic verbal exchange'"*. Students can be prepared for the second element, content, although this is more difficult. Preparing for the defence by preparing answers to typical questions can help here. The component conduct is the most difficult to prepare for *"as it involves complex dynamics and an interesting set of variables"* that is related to the behavior of the committee members. An issue here is the ignorance and misconceptions of students about what to expect. If possible, attending defences of peers can help understand what behavior is expected.

General preparation before the defence

Our advice on preparing for the defence

Preparing yourself for the day of your defence starts days or even weeks in advance. If you are giving a formal presentation you will need to start preparing for it ahead of time, allowing about two to three weeks to make slides, edit your presentation, and practice. Make sure your presentation is ready two to three days before your defence so that you can practice it: by yourself and in front of your friends and colleagues. You can also show it to your supervisor if this is common practice in your department. Learn more about making your presentation in the section "Making your presentation".

You will also want to do a few other concrete things in preparation for your defence, such as re-reading your thesis while highlighting some sentences and making notes, and also re-reading the key papers from your area of research. These can include review articles and high-profile papers. Your preparation can also include reading new research articles that have just been published in your area, to help you stay "on top of the topic". Reading and re-reading your thesis and research articles helps you get your brain working again, especially if you've had a break from your research for some time, and it also gets the topic of your research back on the tip of your tongue: if you have just read your thesis and the relevant articles, it will be much easier to talk about them during your PhD defence, as we've seen in the section "Research insights on preparing for the defence".

Here is the list of things-to-do that one of my (Olga's) coaching clients shared with me, who had only three weeks until her PhD defence:

- finishing writing the papers she'd been working on,
- improving the PowerPoint presentation and rehearsing it,
- identifying and answering questions that would potentially come up during the defence,
- reading new articles on her research topic,
- re-reading older articles where she felt she needed to clarify some aspects,

- reading on the research topics of the two professors who would be on the committee,
- re-reading the thesis.

If you do not have a presentation-type PhD defence but rather an exam-type defence, then you will not need to prepare a presentation and you can just focus on the rest of the items in your preparation.

During the last couple of weeks before the defence you can also organize and do a "mock defence", which is a rehearsal for the real thing. You can find more information on the mock defence in the section "Practicing for the defence".

Former PhD candidates' experiences of preparing for the defence

In the following paragraphs, you can find stories and best practices from former PhD candidates.

Shimabukuro (2018) shares that in addition to preparing for your presentation and the mock *viva*, you can look up types of questions generally asked at defences and prepare answers. You can reread emails and notes from meetings with your committee members, summarize their concerns and pet peeves, and develop answers to address these, as well as note down the associated page numbers of your thesis for reference. Afterwards you can reread your thesis and mark parts with these possible questions in mind. Shimabukuro (2018) prepared for the defence like this – yet nothing that was prepared came up during the defence. However, the thorough preparation helped to build confidence.

Kamal (2019) prepared for the defence like this: first marking up her thesis, and then analyzing the thesis by taking notes in a notebook about each chapter, its main points, and the pages where these points were. She also made a list of standard questions and prepared answers for them.

Similarly, Trueman (2018) spent a considerable amount of time preparing for the defence: rereading the thesis, highlighting key points and buzz words, writing a paragraph on the general argument from each chapter, preparing and practicing answers to general questions with *viva* cards, asking her supervisor to point out the weakest parts of the thesis and practicing justifications, as well as reading additional information on websites and in *viva* preparation books. Even though this kind of preparation may not serve to answering any specific question from your committee during the actual defence, a thorough preparation can still build your confidence and create the right defence mindset.

Other former candidates' opinions on how thoroughly you should prepare are different. As Killen (2017) says: *"I don't think anyone could have prepared me for what happened at the actual defence since committees are unique combinations of scholars"*. Regal (2016) has the following advice:

> If I were to give younger scholars advice on all this it would be, do the work. Let nothing get in the way of doing the work. If you focus on the research and the writing, then it doesn't matter what happens at the defence, you'll be ready. Do not prepare for the defence, simply write your dissertation. Accept that after all this research you know the answers.[2]

Similarly, Abambres (2019) advises you to be confident and not to rehearse your presentation too much. "Not rehearsing too much" means you prepare for your defence presentation as you would prepare for any other presentation. If you have paid attention to developing and mastering your presentation skills and building up your confidence throughout your PhD studies, you will be a much more skilled and confident speaker and presenter as you approach your defence day (see the section "Prepare for your defence by giving talks throughout your PhD"). Not rehearsing too much also means that you should not learn your presentation word for word, by heart, which would make you sound unnatural. You can find more strategies for building your confidence and dealing with anxiety before thesis submission and defence in the section "Dealing with anxiety before thesis submission and defence".

How committee members prepare for the defence

We can also learn more about how to prepare for the defence from what committee members share about how *they* prepare to judge one. Here is an account from an external committee member about how he prepared for a defence by examining the thesis (van Vliet, 2017):

> So once I receive the thesis, I start reading it. I recommend supplying the examiners with a pdf version as well: especially in countries like the UK where the thesis is a phonebook size and weight, and I don't want to carry that around! It may be a courtesy but certainly appreciated. One of the things I look for in a thesis is accessibility: is it easy to understand, is the presentation aimed at making the work accessible, and

is it easy to read? I once had a thesis where all figures were grouped, meaning I sometimes had to go back 50 pages to see a figure - very inconvenient. It is important to realize that the *viva* is confidential, but the thesis will become available. So the only thing that people can view to see what is required for a PhD degree at that university, is the PhD thesis. So the thesis should be of high quality, well presented, as proof that the degrees are earned and not given away easily. Hence comes the need to do a good job, and potential revisions! When I read a thesis, I check whether it gives a good insight in the subject matter, is up to date with the literature, does not look at the data in isolation but also adds context and understanding, and where possible contains a level of speculation/new hypotheses, i.e. takes some risks as well. It is not just a report, it needs to be much more than that. Examiners usually have to write a pre-*viva* report, which is the last chance to delay/stop the *viva* if there are significant issues detected. There needs to be sufficient content, it needs to be of publishable quality, and in the *viva* it needs to be checked whether the student did the work themselves, and if not, whether that is appropriately indicated.

Your committee

Purpose of your committee

The purpose of your committee members (or **examiners**, or **opponents**[3]) is to evaluate if your work is worthy of a doctoral title. Depending on your institution, the involvement of your committee members can be from the start of the project, or only towards your defence. The role of your committee is a function of the defence format – see Chapter 5 for detailed descriptions.

In the United States, for example, committee members are often professors from the same university, who will be involved with the PhD research project from the beginning of the doctoral program. They will attend and examine the proposal of the doctoral candidate and they will generally serve as secondary advisors to the PhD candidate during the PhD trajectory. On the other hand, in the Netherlands, the committee members are selected only when the main supervisor(s) of the PhD candidate have approved the thesis. The committee members then evaluate the thesis and provide questions during the defence.

Regardless of when the committee members start playing a role during the PhD trajectory, their independent review of the thesis and their questions during the PhD defence will determine its course and outcome. At this stage, your supervisor is confident that your work is ready for defending and will take a step aside to let other experts make the final decision.

If you have many meetings with your committee during your doctoral years, the focus is on formative assessment.[4] If your committee mostly evaluates your thesis and then participates during your defence, the focus is on summative assessment[5] (Barnett, Harris, & Mulvany, 2017). The impartial thesis defence that characterizes the European summative assessment conducted by seasoned experts in the specific research field should potentially[6] be more critical than the final thesis committee assessment in the US system. However, as the expectations and understanding of what exactly should be examined during the thesis defence vary widely between European institutions and between individual scientists (especially between generations), there is a wide variation in the standard of the examination, and in the role of the committee members.

Feedback from your committee serves as a review of your work (Brennan, 2019). As such, the remarks from your committee can help you improve your work and eventually help you get published.

Internal committee members

All committees have members from the same department or university as the candidate. Committee members from the same department can be professors who provided you with assistance and additional supervision on particular topics during your research. When the regulations for compiling a committee require the involvement of members from your university but from a different department, then such a committee member may focus more on the overall scientific soundness and contributions of your work, rather than on the depth of your topic. A committee member from a different department at your institution may be referred to as the "cognate" member (Mežek & Swales, 2016).

Depending on the defence procedures of your university, you may have two committees: an internal one, and then an external one. These two committees will be related to a two-step defence: a closed, internal defence and, if the first one is successful, a public defence with external members, see the section "Single-step versus two-step defences".

External committee members

External committee members are experts in your field of research from a different university. If your opinion counts in selecting your external committee members, then discuss this process thoroughly with your supervisor(s) (Brennan, 2019). If you have based your work on the publications of a professor from another university, then this person could be a good pick for serving as external committee member. If you have exchanged good discussions with a professor during conferences or by email during your research, you can honor this involvement by inviting their participation in your committee. Having a well-known academic giving the stamp of approval to your thesis can reflect positively on your reputation (Brennan, 2019). It offers an external validation of the work and helps you to broaden your network of professional contacts (Kyvik, 2014).

In an analysis of the documentation regarding the PhD defence from 20 British universities (Tinkler & Jackson, 2000), the authors identified requirements in three categories for a professional to be part of a defence committee. These requirements are related to:

- academic credentials (requirements in rank and standing for committee members),
- experience (both experience as committee member and experience in your research field), and
- 'independence' (the ability to judge your work without bias).

For requirements regarding academic credentials, you should check the doctoral regulations of your institution. In terms of experience, Watts (2012) cautions that "big names" or famous researchers in your field are not necessarily good committee members and may not always have realistic expectations of what is achievable in a PhD. On the other hand, committee members who have minimal or no prior experience of the process and the appropriate standards to be applied (and by implication are not "big names" in the field) may be too tough in their efforts to be rigorous. This can lead to bad practice on the part of a committee member who may behave as inquisitor, firing off questions and even interrupting answers, creating an atmosphere of confrontation and hostility. In addition, committee members without any formal training or induction in how to conduct the oral examination could have free reign over the process. This situation has the potential for abuse and irregularity. Whilst the evidence of abuse is predominantly anecdotal, some research has identified a number of negative behaviors on the part of committee members: aggression, sarcasm, and hostility, belittling tactics that may humiliate the student, and discriminatory behavior on the ground of gender and race as well as other stereotyping.

The final criterion, i.e. the independence of the external committee member(s) was an important criterion in 19 out of 20 of the universities studied by Tinkler and Jackson (2000). This independence is typically associated with rules in one or more of the following three areas:

1   rules regarding the time period that must have elapsed since the external committee member had a formal attachment to the university of the doctoral candidate,
2   rules that quantify how often the professional can act as a committee member at the university of the doctoral candidate, and
3   rules that determine whether and under what conditions the supervisor can act as a committee member.

Independence should be guaranteed by making sure the committee member has no conflict of interest and can act independently. One should make sure not to recommend family members or close friends to act as your committee members, and you should also check that there are no commercial conflicts of interest, although the latter are not very common in academia. The goal of having rules for the independence of the (external) committee member(s) is to foster impartiality, preserve common academic standards, and develop academic communities (Tinkler & Jackson, 2000). However, given the biases in human nature (Saul, 2013), it is highly debatable whether independent judgement can ever be attained (Stanley & Wise, 1993). At several institutions an external committee member is required to have examined at least three doctorates. This requirement does assure a certain amount of experience among the two committee members. However, this method in turn raises questions about entry into existing networks of committee members, the micropolitics of inclusion and exclusion, and how committee members are chosen via networks, sponsorship and interest representation. Moreover, Kyvik (2014) points out that an external committee member may not want to be critical or negative about a candidate out of "collegiality" for the candidate's supervisor. The examination of doctoral degrees in the UK is left to informal networks and a belief in a notion of collegiality. But "collegiality" is one of those words that often masks complex power relations and the manipulative practices to which these can give rise. The selection of committee members via existing collegiate networks also raises concerns regarding the integrity of the defence as an independent academic process (Watts, 2012).

When your committee includes external committee members, it may be important to remember that serving as a committee member is often a voluntary task.

Professors are busy people and the time they have available to review your thesis and provide feedback may be limited. If it is advised or is customary in the country of your PhD, you might want to go and visit your external committee member(s) before your defence, so that you can explain some parts of your thesis in more detail, and so that you can make sure your committee member reserves some time for you. When time constraints of external committee members pose difficulties in getting thorough feedback on your work, emeritus professors may be able to provide a more in-depth review of it and may be happy to spend more time discussing it with you. I (Eva) had two emeritus professors in my committee who provided very detailed feedback on my thesis and helped take my work to the next (i.e. publishable) level.

Assigned committee

Depending on your institution, you may have a committee assigned to you, or you can be involved in the selection of your committee members. When you are assigned a committee, these committee members may be stakeholders in the project and/or collaborators on the project. Your committee can be a combination of internal and external members. Often, your supervisor will invite these committee members, based on the direction of your research. When you have a committee assigned to you, this assignment often takes place at the beginning of the project – a practice common in the USA. This committee will then be involved with your research at various steps along the way.

In some cases, you may have an external committee associated to your research project, which is not directly the committee that examines you during the defence.

Some research projects require regular feedback from so-called user committees with members from industry or government. Presenting your work at regular intervals during your PhD trajectory to such a committee will help you learn how to listen to questions that come from different perspectives, and how to articulate your answers in a broadly understandable way.

Selecting a committee

If you are involved in the selection of your committee, you can make suggestions to your supervisor about (international) experts on your research topic. If you have the possibility to make such suggestions, you still need to make sure your whole committee fulfils the requirements of the doctoral regulations at your institution. At Delft University of Technology, for example, the doctoral regulations stipulate that the committee should consist of the rector magnificus[7], promotor[8], co-promotor[9], five more members, and a spare member. Then, there are requirements for how many of these members must be full professors, should not have been involved with the research, and should be from outside of Delft University of Technology (TU Delft, 2014). An example of a resulting committee is shown in Figure 4.1. You may need to think for a while before putting together your committee.

If you can be involved with the selection of committee members, provide strategic recommendations. For example, if you want to underline the practical relevance of your work, including a member from industry or government may help you with the formulation of practical recommendations or policy proposals. Their involvement in your committee may then, after your successful

80 *Preparing for your defence*

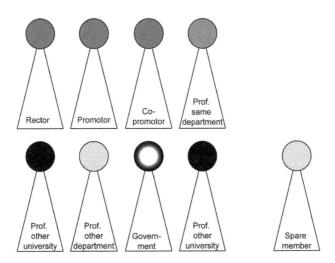

Figure 4.1 Overview of resulting committee according to regulations from Delft University of Technology. The spare member is on call on the day of the defence for emergency replacement of one of the committee members.

defence, bring you one step closer to implementing your work in practice or influencing government policy. Such involvement in your defence committee can follow from having a user committee with members from government and/or industry. According to Tinkler and Jackson (2000), *"The quality of the candidate's examination team is an important indicator of the quality of the resulting degree"*.

Selecting the right committee members can be crucial in avoiding delays in the thesis defence (Yahaghi, Sorooshian, & Yahaghi, 2017). The authors recommend not selecting committee members with a busy schedule, or unprofessional committee members who do not properly prepare for the defence. We want to note here that whether or not a committee member will prepare properly for the defence may be hard to know in advance.

For research projects that are interdisciplinary, it is good practice to make sure that the committee also reflects the different fields relevant to the project. The risk here is that a committee member will examine you as if you are defending in one field only. For such cases, you may want to remind your supervisor to inform committee members of the breadth of your work as opposed to the depth of some stricter single discipline-related studies. From this point of view, (Jacobs, 2018) advises making sure you have a diverse committee, representing different viewpoints and disciplines, to avoid your defence becoming focused on only one single aspect of your work.

Traditionally, the UK-style *viva* is held with the candidate and two committee members (one internal and one external) only. Some universities however add a Chair, who is solely responsible for the procedural part of the defence, and some universities require or allow the supervisors to be present (but not participate in) the defence. If you are able to choose whether your supervisor can be present and you have a good relationship with them, then it is recommended you have them there: *"the supportive presence of a supervisor has both psychological and practical elements and can help moderate the mood of what some students will perceive as a 'gladiatorial' contest"* (Watts, 2012).

Besides all the technical requirements for your committee, you may also be faced with a practical hurdle: making sure you can actually schedule a date for your defence. In some universities, scheduling your defence date is simply a matter of booking a meeting room and finding a time and date when all committee members are available. In other universities, such as for those in the Netherlands, the strict protocol related to doctoral defences puts restrictions on the possible time slots. In fact, when I (Eva) put together my committee, I ended up having to change one committee member as it was easier to replace that one than to find another timeslot to defend my thesis in the only room allowed for defences in Delft.

Preparing for committee feedback

To prepare for feedback from your committee, you should try to see your thesis from the perspective of the committee members. As such, you need to know your committee members (and thus their work) well. As you prepare for your defence, don't make the mistake of focusing only on your own dissertation. Take a step back and evaluate your work through the eyes of your committee members. Check out their most recent publications so you are fully up-to-date; you don't want to be uninformed when a committee member hints at the fact that they worked on something relevant to your research very recently. Don't assume that you have read everything while writing your dissertation; check out the latest and in press publications and preprints of your committee members.

Some committee members will tell you their exam questions in advance, which will allow you to come to the defence with additional material. Other members won't give you any idea of how they will evaluate your thesis. If you haven't had a chance to meet your committee member before the defence, ask people who know them about how they tend to examine and which topics are of particular interest to them.

Making your presentation

Presenting for your audience

Most defence formats use some form of a presentation. In practice, this means that part of your defence preparation will include making a (digital) presentation; often either a sequence of slides (for example, Microsoft PowerPoint slides), a more organic walkthrough of your work (for example, a Prezi presentation), or a short summary statement at the beginning without backup tools. We will leave the choice of software for designing your presentation up to you and will focus here on sharing general concepts for preparing the content of your presentation.

If you are to give an opening statement without any backup material, then your preparation may look a bit different from what is described below. In that case, you can make a mind map of the most important aspects of your work: background, research question, methods, results, broader implications, and conclusions. If you like, you can write out your speech and practice your timing. You can send the typed-out version of your speech to your supervisor for input. If you prefer to practice only by speaking through your speech, you may want to use your mind map for reference during the first trial runs and then gradually practice without any support. In this case, set up a meeting with your supervisor to practice your opening statement and get feedback.

For the rest of this section, we'll assume that you are giving a full presentation with projected material. To make sure you are well-prepared for your presentation, start working on it in advance. Make a plan which allows for all the steps necessary in the process. Include time for your supervisor to send feedback and allow some breathing space in your planning. Figure 4.2 shows a flowchart of the steps in preparing for your presentation, with a possible plan. One possible step is "extra calculations": you may want to develop some additional graphs to project during your defence or make a last-minute calculation to address a possible question.

84 *Preparing for your defence*

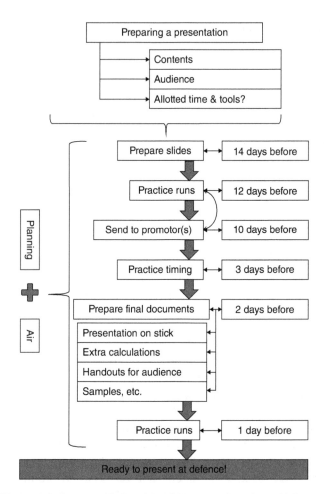

Figure 4.2 Steps and planning of your presentation. "Air" stands for breathing space in your planning.

The content of your presentation depends on your audience. Before you start working on your presentation, identify who you are presenting to during your defence.

Are you presenting to the general public? Is your committee purely academic? Do you have committee members from industry or government?

In the Netherlands, a defence starts with a presentation for the general public. This presentation does not form part of the actual defence with the committee and the public does not ask questions – its purpose is to inform friends and family who attend the defence about your work. Other defence formats can use the presentation as the cornerstone of the defence with the order and the contents of the questions being organized around the presentation. If you haven't had a chance to attend a defence at your university (for example if all defences are closed to the public), then confirm with your supervisor and a recent PhD graduate from your program who will be in the audience for your presentation.

Once you have identified your audience, you can select the focus of your presentation. If you are presenting to the general public, you need to spend more time explaining the background of your work, why your research matters, and what are the broader implications of your findings. If you present only to a committee of professors in a narrow field of research, then your audience may be fully aware of the background of your research. A quick summary is then sufficient, after which you can delve more into the details.

One more tip for when you start drafting your presentation: it is helpful to enquire how much time is given for your presentation and then decide on the number of slides. My (Olga's) advice would be to have one slide per minute as I like to change my slides often to keep my presentations lively and flowing. However, this will depend on your style of presentation or the style accepted at your department or in your field of studies.

Summarizing your work

When you've spent three, four, or even more years on your research, you may feel tempted to try and fit everything you did during your PhD studies into your defence presentation. However, when you reach your defence, what matters most is your research question and how you answered it. Structure your presentation around the most important findings of your work.

Present the evidence that helped you formulate the answer to your research question, as well as contradictory evidence if you found that in the literature, or if some of your findings (seem to) indicate something different. If you have contradictory evidence, make sure you have a plausible explanation. Where appropriate, you can indicate that further (experimental) research may be needed to clarify certain aspects. These parts, however, should be side notes – the evidence for the answer to your research question should be sound enough to be a likely explanation.

To structure your presentation, there are two formats you can use as a starting point: the scientific method approach, and the mathematical proof approach (Lantsoght, 2018a). The scientific method approach contains (roughly) the following elements:

- overview slide,
- background or literature review,
- methods (experiments or calculations),
- results and analysis,
- discussion (of the results, with comparisons to existing literature),
- conclusions.

The mathematical proof approach is structured as follows:

- overview slide,
- hypothesis,
- methods used to prove hypothesis,
- actual proof,
- consequences,
- outlook.

For your doctoral defence presentation, you can fill in these building blocks of the presentation as follows:

- **Overview slide:** Start your presentation with one slide that shows the outline of your presentation. Using an overview slide will help your audience understand the structure of your presentation (type of presentation that they can expect), as well as identify the building blocks of your presentation and the main approach you followed (are you presenting experimental work, numerical work, theoretical analysis?). You can use your overview slide to mention the "Take Home Message" for the first time (i.e., the most important message of your presentation, which every person in the audience should remember at the end of your presentation, see Figure 4.3(a)).
- **Background or literature review:** Before you delve into your research, spend enough time sketching the broader field and what has been done before. Use the background and literature review to show the knowledge gaps that exist in your field. Moreover, the beginning of your presentation is a good time to explain why your research matters. How did your work make a tiny dent in the universe and how can your work serve to advance society as a whole? Here is where you have an opportunity to show your audience why they should

care about your work. Figure 4.3(b) shows an example of how to frame research within the broader scope of society from the viewpoint of sustainability. This is also the right place to review the literature and refer to the most relevant papers published by others in your field. You can refer to a few individual papers and, optionally, summarize their findings in a graph or a table. After having introduced the existing gaps in your field of studies, you can state your research question.

- **Methods:** How did you study your research question? Did you use experimental, numerical, or analytical methods? Describe the methods that you used. As much as possible, show photographs and videos of your methods. A time-lapse of different stages of your methods (for example, preparation and execution of experiments, or sped-up walkthrough of procedures of numerical experiment) can be informative for your audience to show the "how" of your research.[10]
- **Results and analysis:** What did you find? You can answer this question in two steps: 1) What was the outcome of your methods; and 2) What was the outcome of the analysis of your methods? Present your material in such a way that it leads to answers to your research question. Try to use graphs rather than tables, as they are easier for your audience to understand. You may have done additional experiments and analyses, but if they were of minor importance, they should not be the focus of your presentation. Remember that your presentation should not be an account of your past years as a researcher, but a story about your research question and your proposed answer to that question.
- **Discussion**: This section is to discuss the meaning of your results and to put them into the context of existing studies. Do it by comparing them to the literature

Preparing for your defence 89

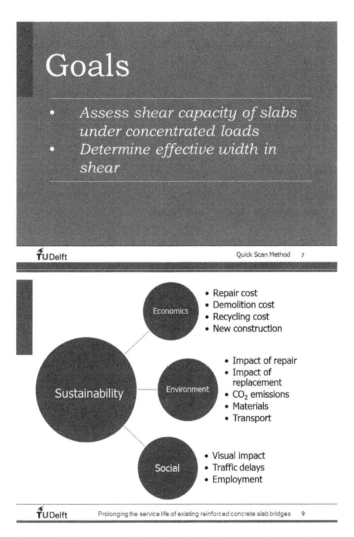

Figure 4.3 Example slides: (a) slide with research question or goals of research, (b) Linking research to broader scope and impact on society as a whole.

and putting your findings into the broader context. You can also address how your findings fit into the current theories and understanding or how your work implies developments or changes to these.
- **Conclusions:** What's the "Take Home Message" of your work? Focus on this message, which should be a one-sentence summary of your proposed answer to your research question. Round off your presentation by summarizing the background (Why does your research matter? Which gap did you identify that required further study?), the methods (How did you address your research question?), your results (What did you observe?) and discussion (How did you interpret these observations?). Avoid using too much text here.
- **Hypothesis:** If you use the presentation style that follows a mathematical proof, then you first show your hypothesis and then your proof. Instead of presenting your research question, you present your proposed answer. If your presentation is for the general public and/or includes industry participants or government employees, you may want to go one step further: present (policy) recommendations as your hypothesis, and then go through your supporting evidence for these recommendations. If you present recommendations, then your research should have included looking at practical case studies and be oriented towards (direct) implementation. Make sure to include the steps in developing evidence in this section.
- **Methods used to prove hypothesis:** see "Methods" above.
- **Actual proof:** Go through the evidence gathered with your described methods. Show how this evidence supports your hypothesis. Be thorough in developing your proof, but at the same time focus on visual information. You can use the same material here as you would

use in the "Results" section of the scientific method approach presentation, but the way you organize your talk should be different. Here, you focus on walking the audience through your evidence, instead of first presenting what you observed and then how you explain those observations.
- **Consequences:** If your work had a more theoretical approach and you centered your presentation on the answer to your research question, you can address possible (policy) recommendations in this part of your research. You can identify further (case) studies that may be necessary before implementation of your ideas can be recommended. If your work has already included (policy) recommendations, then you can sketch here the expected effect of your proposal.
- **Outlook:** Repeat your hypothesis. Then identify which (minor) topics still need to be addressed and sketch how you see the continuation of your topic of research (for a future generation of PhD students).

Let's repeat this again: the focus of your presentation should be your research question and your proposed answer to that question. If you are doubtful whether you should include something, ask yourself: "Does this contribute to answering my research question?" If yes, include it. If no, remove it. If you are in doubt, add it as a backup slide after your final slide, so that you can bring it up if somebody asks a question that requires showing this information as evidence.

Other forms of visual information

If your defence format does not include a presentation, it still may be wise to prepare some form of visual information to support your replies to the questions of your committee members. You could think of bringing the following to your defence:

- a small-scale mock-up of your experimental setup,
- something from the lab, such as a sample of the material you used, a test specimen, etc.,
- photographs of your experimental work, field work, etc.,
- sketches that illustrate the concepts of your theoretical work,
- a mind map or general structure flowchart of how you organized your research,
- a poster with relevant information.

If you have an idea to bring something to your defence, and it is not common in your university to do so, check with your supervisor and the office of doctoral regulations to confirm that you are allowed to bring in extra material during your defence.

Tips for presenting

In this section, you will find some practical tips to help you be a better and more confident presenter. Ideally, you work on your presentation skills throughout your entire PhD trajectory. From that perspective, we recommend the following:

- **Practice before presenting**: Practice your presentation out loud and use a stopwatch to measure your timing. Compare the measured time to the allotted time. If you go over time, then remove content from your presentation. Don't solve this issue by speeding up your speech. Setting aside the time to practice your presentation means that you have to make it ahead of time, so that you can practice and course-correct where needed. I (Eva) usually practice my presentation at least three times: once when developing my draft slide deck to check if I'm on time (often weeks before the event), a second time to check if my modified presentation is on time, and a third time the day before the event.

- **Present often:** Take the opportunity to present your work wherever possible, including conferences and group and lunch time seminars. Addressing questions from any audience functions as training for addressing committee questions during your defence. Present to different audiences and learn to adapt your presentation to these different circumstances.
- **Reflect on your presentations:** I (Eva) strongly recommend self-reflection. After each and every presentation you make, take a moment to reflect on your presentation. You can develop this reflection in your (research) diary, or through a blog post (Lantsoght, 2010). Answer the following questions for yourself: *What went well? Did I stay on time? What would I improve for the next presentation? How did I feel before, during, and after the presentation? Did something or somebody make me nervous?* When you prepare your next presentation, read through your evaluation and use these insights to improve.
- **Formulas:** Avoid showing formulas in your presentation. Only show formulas if you are going to use them as an important part of your evidence. If you show a formula, walk your audience through all inputs and outputs and symbols used in the expression. You can

use animations to bring up circles to direct the attention of your audience to the parameter that you want to discuss.
- **Visual information:** Avoid large amounts of text in presentations. Keep your information as visual as possible. For every drawing that you present, simplify it to show a version that is as pure and as easy to grasp as possible.
- **Walk your audience through graphs**: If you show results and/or analysis of results, show graphs rather than tables. When you bring up a graph, explain it thoroughly to your audience. Don't make the mistake of saying "and here are my results" and then moving on to the next topic. Explain to the audience what you show on the x- and y-axes of your graph. Explain what the datapoints represent and give a quick comment on how the datapoints relate to your methods (i.e. how did you obtain these datapoints?). Then, state what you observe from these datapoints (i.e. how do you interpret these outcomes?).
- **Research question or take-home message on separate slide:** To draw the attention of your audience to either your research question or its answer (i.e. main hypothesis), you can make a separate slide with a short sentence (or keywords) in large font with a background of a different color to the rest of your presentation. Then, you can bring up this slide a number of times during your presentation to make sure your audience will get the key point. Figure 4.3(b) shows an example of a slide with the goals of the research, which serves to define the research question.

If English is not your native language, and your defence be held in English, you face the challenge of presenting in a language that is not your own.[11] If the language itself is a cause of stress and anxiety, work on improving your spoken language skills. Ask for help and training in your university if you need it. Practice as often as possible. Immerse yourself in the language by listening to podcasts, reading English books, or attending an English-speaking summer school. To prepare for your defence presentation, find a critical friend who can help you with the difficult words in your presentation before the defence. If you don't feel comfortable about your language skills, don't brush the issue to one side. Acknowledge the situation and then see what you can do to get the training and support you need to get to a level where you don't notice language as a barrier anymore. In the section "Language-related difficulties with questions", you will find research insights concerning the defence for non-native English speakers.

Here are additional resources about doing a presentation and making it a great one: *Marketing for Scientists* by Marc Kuchner (2011), all books by Edward Tufte on showing visual information (Tufte, 1990, 1997, 2001, 2006), *Better Presentations* by Jonathan Schwabisch (Schwabisch, 2016), *Championing Science* by Roger and Amy Aines for presenting to decision-makers (Aines & Aines, 2019), and *Virtual Engagement* by Ernie Mendes to improve your virtual presentations (Mendes, 2020).

How to prepare for committee questions

Before your defence, prepare a list of possible questions that may be asked by your committee members and prepare answers to them (Brennan, 2019). You can find lists of *viva* questions on the web (for example: University of Leicester, 2020; NDPH Student blog, 2017; Broad, 2020) and below you will find suggestions and inspiration for compiling your own list. If possible, prepare for answering questions by organizing a mock defence (Brennan, 2019). See the section "Practicing for the defence" for more on using a mock defence to practice.

When preparing for your defence, ask yourself the following questions related to your contribution, your ability to carry out research, and the implications of your findings: "*What has my research contributed to my field? What are my new findings?*" While your contribution should be presented clearly in your thesis, you will need to state it during your defence. Depending on the amount of interaction you had with your committee members before the defence, your answers may clarify aspects of your research process and clear up any misunderstandings (Watts, 2012).

If you have a large committee, as is common in parts of continental Europe, where each member of the committee gets to ask perhaps only one question, you may find yourself speculating what The Question of Committee Member Y could be. To get a better idea of what to expect, get to know your committee members as suggested in the section "Your committee". Send your thesis to them weeks in advance. If it is a custom in your country or university, go to hand in your thesis to a committee member personally and use the opportunity to have a quick chat about your thesis. Plan formal meetings with them to discuss it.

Wellington (2010) collected exam questions from 23 vivas where he served as external committee member and a comparable number where he served as an internal committee member. His conclusion is that the general questions are largely predictable, but not the specific questions particular to one's thesis. His list of questions is as follows (note that some of these questions would only apply to certain fields of study and are not universal to all types of research):

- *General*
    - *Motivation: what made you do this piece of research? Why did you choose this topic? Why do you think it is important?*
    - *Position: What is your own position (professional or personal) in relation to this field and these research questions? What prior conceptions and/or experiences did you bring to this study? How did your own position/background/bias affect your data analysis and your data collection?*
    - *Contribution: please could you summarize your thesis? What are the main findings of your research? What would somebody from this field learn from reading your thesis that they didn't know before? What did you learn from doing it? What original contribution to knowledge do you feel that you have made?*
    - *Publication: which elements of your work do you feel are worthy of publication and/or presentation at a conference? What plans do you have for publication and dissemination? Has any of the work been published or presented already?*
- *Theories and theoretical frameworks*
    - *Please talk us through the main research questions that you were trying to address in your work. What was the origin of these questions?*
    - *What theories/theoretical frameworks/perspectives have you drawn upon in your research?*
    - *Which theories did your study illuminate, if any?*

- *Literature review*
  - *What shaped or guided your literature review? Why did it cover the areas that it did (and not others)? Why did/didn't you include the work of X in your study?*
- *On methodology and analysis of data*
  - *Methodology: why did you employ the methods you used? Why not others, e.g. X? What informed your choice of methods? What would you do differently, with hindsight? What ethical issues arose before, during and after the research?*
  - *The Sample: why did you select this sample? Can you see any problems with it? If it is a small-scale study, can you justify why so few were involved?*
  - *Data analysis: did anything surprise you in the data ("hit you in the face")? Any anomalies? How did you analyze your data? How did you categorize/filter the data? Did themes emerge from your data (a posteriori) or did you "bring them to the data" (a priori)? Why did you analyze it in this way? Could it have been done in another way?*
  - *Further work: which aspects of the work could be taken further? How?*
- *Generalizability and key messages*
  - *How far do think you can generalize from your work? What lessons can be learnt from it by practitioners/policy makers/other researchers? The "so what" question: what are its key messages and implications?*
- *Open forum.*
  - *Reflections on the thesis: what are its strengths? And its limitations or weaknesses (with hindsight)? Is there anything else you would like to say or discuss that we have not asked you about?*

Use the above list, as well as the referenced lists online, to prepare for your defence and committee questions. Discuss possible answers with your peers and friends in the time leading up to your defence. In case of doubt, discuss with your supervisor. The more you talk about it, the easier it will be to come up with some answers during your defence when the pressure is high.

Make sure that your presentation materials are at least adequate, as discussed in the section "Making your presentation", and that you present confidently. If you put some effort into making your slides excellent, your audience, including the committee members, will notice your material as well as your articulate presentation. If you tend to freeze up when asked questions, you might want to work on this particular area during your PhD and in the time leading up to the defence: practice potential defence questions with friends, and practice presenting throughout your PhD trajectory.

Back in the time when I (Olga) got my PhD degree (it was in 2003), it was ok to present an experimental study without diving too much into the details of the theoretical background, or how the study is going to impact it. Theoretical explanation was left to the theoreticians. Now the times are changing and it is increasingly expected that you will have a grasp of the impact of your experimental studies on the theory, and that you will even have done some theoretical work yourself in addition to the experimental results you have obtained. Make sure you know what is currently expected in your field and that, when preparing for your committee questions, you can articulate whether your research involves any theoretical studies or predictions, and incorporates current theories or even advances them.

If your work is purely theoretical, practice to describe how your results extend current theories or even create a breakthrough in the state-of-the-art. If your work is purely experimental, make sure you highlight that data collection formed a major part of your study and, if it involved a sophisticated or novel method, you should spotlight that in your answers.

If your work has a potential claim to be Intellectual Property, practice in advance how you would describe it in front of the committee members.

Furthermore, let us have a look at the guidelines used for the assessment of the defence. Knowing those guidelines can help you prepare yourself for the questions even better. Note that grading rubrics are not commonly used but some universities are moving towards their use in an attempt to standardize the assessment of the defence. To guide committee members in the assessment of PhD theses and defences, (Vaccari & Thangam, 2010) developed a grading rubric which evaluates all technical aspects of the work, as well as the potential for Intellectual Property and performance during the defence. Based on these rubrics, we can identify the following areas that you want to pay attention to when preparing for your defence.

- **Originality and novelty of your research:**[12] Make sure you are able to articulate this if asked by one of the committee members: is it an extension of the previous work? Does it improve on previous approaches? Has it produced results with a high impact?
- **Advancement of the state-of-the-art in your research area:** Have your results incrementally advanced the knowledge or methodology in your field of research? Can the results be expected to have a moderate impact? If the results have produced a major impact, make sure you can articulate it.

- **Practical and/or academic utility**: Reflect on how the results of your work can be used by others in applications or in further research studies. For example, did you do experiments that others can use to test their theories and models? Did you develop policy recommendations or tools that can be used in practice?
- **Use of new and advanced methods:** Make sure you are able to describe the methods you used in your research and explain whether they are standard in your area, advanced, or even leading-edge, not applied before in this research field.

Dealing with anxiety before thesis submission and defence

Tight stomach, extreme anxiety, fear that it is not going to be good enough, not wanting to submit, delaying and procrastinating, not being able to face the thesis: you might be experiencing some or all of this before your thesis submission and defence.

It might sound awful, but the reality is that ... this anxiety is experienced by those who defended their thesis in flying colors and with no corrections, by those who passed their thesis with minor corrections, and by those who passed their thesis with major corrections. This anxiety is something universal and you are feeling it because it is natural to feel it before thesis submission and defence. It does not mean that you are not good enough, that you have not done enough to deserve the PhD title, or that you will fail your thesis. It means that you are nearing the end of the magnificent and difficult undertaking of doing your PhD. Putting it all into one document (your thesis) that will be rigorously checked as well as putting yourself out there for evaluation during your defence is naturally scary. It would be strange if you did not feel that anxiety.

The question is not whether you will be anxious before the thesis submission and defence, because you will be! The real question is how are you not going to let this anxiety ruin your productivity and well-being during these crucial last weeks or months. Here are some strategies to help you deal with this anxiety.

Dealing with anxiety before the thesis submission

There might be a period of several months that signifies the "before the submission" era in your PhD journey. You are working hard, writing chapters of your thesis, sending them to your supervisor, receiving corrections, revising, editing and proofreading. A lot of other things in your work and life are put on hold.

Like many of the PhD students among my (Olga's) clients, you also might be plagued by worries and negative thoughts that discourage you and make you feel anxious. Thoughts such as: "It is not going to be good enough", "I have not done enough", "It needs more work before I can submit", "I don't know enough", "My writing is not good enough", "It will be criticized", "I won't be able to explain it at the defence", "I am going to fail", and so on and so on … You might be worrying whether you and your work deserve a PhD title, and whether it is going to be liked and accepted by the committee members.

Particularly in the last weeks and days before the submission, you might be even more anxious. You will feel increasingly tired from constantly writing, editing and proofreading your thesis. You might be feeling overwhelmed as you realize that there is still more to do than there is time left before your submission date. This tiredness and feeling of being overwhelmed will fuel your anxiety about the submission. You might feel as if you cannot possibly look at your thesis any more and cannot face editing and proofreading it again. You might be overwhelmed by last minute formatting of text, figures and tables. Thoughts of giving up and not submitting and walking away from it all because you "just cannot do it" might be going through your head. All of this is **normal and common**.

You might be looking at your thesis through a perfectionist's eyes, so remind yourself to be less of a perfectionist and to focus on the absolutely necessary minimum. Ask yourself: "**What can you not submit your thesis without**?" Focusing on those tasks and making sure you follow the formal requirements for thesis formatting and submission can help tame your anxiety. If you wanted to add many more things to your thesis but you are running out of time, remember that, probably, no one knows about those things and you can skip them safely. Focusing on bringing your thesis into submittable form is much more important at this stage than putting in all the things you had in mind. You will need to let go of some of your ideas, no matter how painful it might be. A good thesis is a submitted thesis! Remember that there will still be time for corrections following the defence or the comments of the committee members.

Here is what one of my (Olga's) clients shared about how she dealt with the anxiety before thesis submission.

> I needed to remind myself that there still will be *viva* and thesis corrections. The thesis will be

read and corrected by someone, and it will be improved. So, I don't need to continue torturing myself making it absolutely perfect as it will still be corrected by someone and I will have a chance to implement those corrections.

Dealing with anxiety before the thesis defence

There will probably be several months between your thesis submission and the defence. This means there will be plenty of time for anxiety after your thesis submission before you defend it.

During this time, you might be feeling post-submission blues. This is when you feel low, lost or even depressed after a period of very intense work, and also after years of working hard on your PhD. You are not alone in having post-submission blues. I (Olga) was hit hard by them for several weeks right after submitting my thesis. In the section "Celebrating your achievement" you will see that 42% of the participants of a Twitter poll experienced the blues after finishing their PhD (Lantsoght, 2018b). Treating yourself to a special outing or celebration to mark the occasion, taking time off, or even going on a holiday after your thesis submission and before the defence can help you deal with post-submission blues.

Let's discuss the anxiety that comes up before the defence date, in the last weeks and days leading up to it. During this time, you might fear that you will fail the defence, or that your presentation will go wrong. You might fear the committee questions and be paralyzed by anxiety that you would not be able to answer some of their questions. If you are having a public defence with your colleagues and friends coming, you might be anxious about being exposed in front of them, you might fear them judging you, judging how much you know, and judging your presentation skills. You might be worrying about certain difficulties with your research or challenges with interpretation of your results that you have experienced during your studies. You fear that it will come up during the defence and you won't be able to explain it. You might feel that you have not done enough during your PhD or you should have done it better or faster. You might have an acute feeling of not deserving the title of PhD.

It might be that you are particularly anxious about meeting a certain person during your PhD defence: this might be an external committee member of high caliber who is notorious for asking lots of difficult questions. Or it might be a person from your department, a supervisor or a colleague, with whom you have a taxing relationship.

The worst-case scenario of you failing your defence keeps going through your head and the anxiety levels keep rising higher and higher. I (Eva) had repeated nightmares about my supervisor forgetting to show up for my defence. I don't know how many times I reminded him which day and what time he had to be there – just in case.

This anxiety before your defence can manifest itself in a sick feeling in your stomach (many PhD students have had this). You might not be able to face your thesis anymore: you know that you need to re-read it in preparation for the defence but you cannot look at it anymore because you've had enough. You might not want to go to the defence and feel like you just want to run away and hide.

The good news is that there is a set of tools that has helped many PhD students already and will hopefully help you reduce this anxiety and feel more calm, present and confident.

First of all, let us remind you what the PhD degree is given for: it is given to you if you are able to demonstrate in your thesis and your defence that you can conduct an independent research project (Phillips & Pugh, 2010). So, if you are worried that your research was not novel enough or not enough of a breakthrough, stop worrying about that and start focusing on demonstrating that you have conducted research independently (for more on the definition of originality, see the section "Originality").

The second thing is that the most probable outcome is that you will pass your PhD defence: 24% pass without corrections, 63% with minor corrections, 8% with major corrections and 5% report that they failed (Lantsoght, 2020). It might be that you will be requested to do some minor corrections; it might be that you will be asked to do some major corrections. However, do not worry about the corrections just now: you will deal with these later on. It might even be that you pass with flying colors and no corrections. However, many PhD students before their defence imagine the worst-case scenario, that most probably will not come true, of failing their PhD defence. Here is an alternative suggestion for you: start imagining the best-case scenario of your PhD defence; this practice will calm down your nerves and can be fun as well.

Another thing that I (Olga) have observed in many PhD students among my coaching clients is that they did not believe that they deserved their PhD degree. As a result of this, they felt a lot of anxiety on the run up to and on the day of their PhD defence. How can I convince them that the most probable outcome of their PhD defence is "pass" if they do not even believe they deserve to pass? Ask yourself this question: do you believe that you deserve the PhD degree? If you answer "No", you need to start working on your mindset and change it to believing that you do deserve it:

> I deserve to receive the PhD degree, I have done a lot of hard work, I have written papers and chapters of my PhD thesis, I have done an extensive and independent research project, and even if not everything went smoothly and there have been difficulties, and there are still some outstanding questions, I am ready to receive the PhD title and move on from this chapter of my life.

Going into the PhD defence believing that you deserve the title of PhD will give you confidence and will help you deal with anything that might come up during the defence.

To battle anxiety during the weeks and days coming up to your defence, it is also very important to rest, and get some fresh air and exercise. Good sleep and good rest during the day, such as an afternoon nap or watching a good movie or reading a good (non-scientific) book are all excellent things for contributing to your well-being. Getting some fresh air and exercising are proven to help combat low moods, so some gentle strolls or jogging outside can help you feeling less anxious.

Going away for a couple of days to change your surroundings and do something different can also help to deal with anxiety and low mood. What are the hobbies that you have forgotten and would like to take up now? That can fit well into preparation for your defence.

Here is what one of my (Olga's) clients shared about trying to stay on top of negative thoughts as the defence approached:

> This is not the end of my life. I need to face it with what I have and what I know. If [during the defence] something bad happens, then so be it. In this moment, I need to prepare myself as much as I can.

She also shared that the thought of moving on with her work and life after the defence was helpful.

One more piece of advice for dealing with anxiety has to do with the defence being the end of a big period of your life and the grief and sadness you might be experiencing because of it, without even realizing it. Your PhD defence signifies the end of a huge part of your life, the whole era of you being a PhD student that has lasted so far from three to six years, and in some cases, especially if you have been doing it part-time, up to ten years. Going to the PhD defence will mean the official and imminent end of this era and can cause you huge anxiety. It is important to recognize that and allow for the process of grieving at this period of your life and for letting go of it. Your whole identity will change: you've labeled and perceived yourself as a "PhD student" for many years, and soon you would not be that any more. You will need to find yourself and re-define yourself anew. This can be difficult. Allow your mind to process the situation and, if you are struggling with it, reach out to someone to talk about it. You can help yourself by thinking over the positive aspects and periods of your PhD, by acknowledging the difficulties you overcame, by saying goodbye to them, starting to detach yourself from them, and by imagining new possibilities that you would like to see opening up for your future.

Learn more about dealing with anxiety by reading these books: *You can heal your life* by Louise Hay (1984),

You are not alone by Zachary Westerbeck (2020), *Rewire your anxious brain* by Caroline Pittman and Elizabeth Karle (2015), or *Mindfulness for beginners* by Jon Kabat-Zinn (2016).

Practicing for the defence

As mentioned in the section "Making your presentation", you should practice your presentation a number of times to make sure your timing fits the allotted timeslot. Additionally, practice your presentation for other people: your supervisor, family members, colleagues ... (Shields, 2018).

One of the topics (Watts, 2012) pays attention to is the trial defence, often referred to as the mock defence or mock *viva*. At some universities, it is common to have a mock *viva* (Trueman, 2018). It can help you identify the areas you are uncomfortable with, and for which you can improve your answers. The "mock defence" or "mock *viva*" is used to help the PhD student prepare for the real defence. It can consist of the practice run of your presentation in front of the research group, and answering the questions fired at students by supervisor and colleagues. It can also be an interrogation of the student by their supervisor and colleagues about their thesis, or an oral examination on a small section of the thesis. Usually, participants would aim to imitate as closely as possible the type and content of the defence that is normal in their particular department as well as imitating the defence setting. The section "How to prepare for committee questions" contains many suggestions for compiling possible committee questions to practice for the defence, and these can be used in your mock defence.

Many doctoral candidates have some experience of oral examination as part of either or both earlier undergraduate and postgraduate programs, but a trial run of the defence can be valuable. Watts (2012) studied how such a trial run prepares students for the real thing. Anecdotal evidence shows that many students find the practice useful. Even though students are frequently asked different questions during the mock and the real defence, the mock defence is useful as it allows you to experience "typical" defence arrangements and you get to practice debating your work. It requires, however, a lot of effort to set up a mock defence and, if it is to be beneficial, it must be taken seriously and enacted in a sufficiently rigorous way. Even though the "trial run" cannot fully prepare the candidate or protect them from "unpredictable moments" during the defence, it can help build the student's confidence about the dynamics and challenges of the process. The trial defence may be especially useful for students who are not native speakers of the languages used in the defence.

Manidis and Addo (2017) describe Addo's practice and final defence presentation. The goal of the work is to provide information on presenting knowledge in a formal academic setting. For this purpose, they compared the trial run and final delivery of the defence presentation. The trial run was in the presence of other doctoral candidates who gave feedback on content and delivery. It is important to practice and refine research presentations because the delivery thereof is a learning crucible for almost all doctoral candidates. The final observation of the paper is that: *"Amidst the pressure of today's increasingly public research context, participating, in practice, as practice, through practice, has become a pedagogical imperative"*.

From these insights, we can conclude that it is beneficial to include some form of practice of your defence, whether this be a full mock defence or giving your presentation to your peers.

Notes

1 The *laudatio* is a closing speech from the promotor in praise of the candidate.
2 Note that this former PhD student defended in the US, where the time between thesis submission and defence may be very short in order to finish within a certain semester.
3 We will explain the terminology used in different countries in Chapter 5 and have opted to use "committee" and "committee members" throughout this book for consistency. Note that the role of committee members is different from the role of the opponent or external examiner in some defence formats.
4 Formative assessment is assessment that is considered part of the learning process. Examples of formative assessment typically include homework exercises that serve the sole purpose of practicing concepts, or draft reports on which the instructor gives feedback.
5 Summative assessment evaluates the extent to which the student has reached the intended learning objectives. Summative assessment is the final step and comes after the entire learning process. Examples of summative assessment are final exams or final project reports.
6 This depends on the level of involvement of the committee in the research. In some cases, only the supervisor(s) guide the candidate during the study years and the committee only steps in at the end to examine the thesis and participate in the defence.
7 University president (US), chancellor (Commonwealth).
8 Supervisor/advisor, with *"ius promovendi"*.
9 Co-supervisor. The co-promotor does not need to have *"ius promovendi"*.
10 If you read this book at the early stage of your PhD trajectory, remember to take all necessary photographs and videos of your methods.
11 The same holds true, of course, for languages other than English. It is the non-nativeness that adds an extra challenge.

12 If the word "originality" causes you anxiety, check what we discuss in the section "Originality": the most important aspect is that you can carry out an independent research project. If your work is not a major breakthrough, there is no cause for concern if you can show that you are able to carry out research independently.

References

Abambres, M. (2019). *PhD defenses around the world: A defense in Portugal*. https://www.evalantsoght.com/2019/03/phd-defenses-around-the-world-a-defense-in-portugal.html

Aines, R., & Aines, A. (2019). *Championing science: Communicating your ideas to decision makers*. Oakland, CA: University of California Press.

Barnett, J. V., Harris, R. A., & Mulvany, M. J. (2017). A comparison of best practices for doctoral training in Europe and North America. *FEBS Open Bio, 7*(10): 1444–1452.

Brennan, N. (2019). 100 PhD rules of the game to successfully complete a doctoral dissertation. *Accounting, Auditing & Accountability Journal, 32*(1): 364–376.

Broad, A. (2020). *Nasty PhD viva questions*. https://pages.cpsc.ucalgary.ca/~saul/wiki/uploads/Chapter1/NastyPhDQuestions.html

de-Miguel, M. (2010). The evaluation of doctoral thesis. A model proposal. *RELIEVE: Revista Electrónica de Investigación y Evaluación Educativa, 16*(1): 1–17.

Hay, L. (1984). *You can heal your life*. Carlsbad, CA: Hay House Inc.

Jacobs, S. (2018). *PhD defenses around the world: I passed and you will too*. https://www.evalantsoght.com/2018/12/phd-defenses-around-the-world-i-passed-and-you-will-too.html

Kabat-Zinn, J. (2016). *Mindfulness for beginners: Reclaiming the present moment and your life.* Louisville, CO: Sounds True Publishers.

Kamal, A. (2019). *PhD defenses around the world: A viva in linguistics from England*. https://www.evalantsoght.com/2019/05/phd-defenses-around-the-world-a-viva-in-linguistics-from-england.html

Killen, M. (2017). *PhD defenses around the world: A defense in Education in the USA*. https://www.evalantsoght.com/2017/12/phd-defenses-around-the-world-a-defense-in-education-in-the-usa.html

Kuchner, M. J. (2011). *Marketing for scientists: How to shine in tough times*. Washington, DC: Island Press.

Kyvik, S. (2014). Assessment procedures of Norwegian PhD theses as viewed by examiners from the USA, the UK and Sweden. *Assessment & Evaluation in Higher Education, 39*(2): 140–153.

Preparing for your defence 113

Lantsoght, E. (2010). *Evaluation of my presentation*. https://www.evalantsoght.com/2010/12/evaluation-of-my-presentation.html

Lantsoght, E. O. L. (2018a). *The A-Z of the PhD trajectory – A practical guide for a successful journey*. Cham: Springer.

Lantsoght, E. (2018b). *The post-PhD blues*. https://www.evalantsoght.com/2018/10/the-post-phd-blues.html

Lantsoght, E. (2020). *The outcome of the PhD defense*. https://www.evalantsoght.com/2020/02/the-outcome-of-the-phd-defense.html

Manidis, M., & Addo, R. (2017). Learning a practice through practise: Presenting knowledge in doctoral spoken presentations. *Studies in Continuing Education, 39*(3): 235–250.

Mendes, E. (2020). *Virtual Engagement: For all online presentations, trainings, and meetings*. Independently Published.

Mežek, Š., & Swales, J. M. (2016). PhD defences and vivas. In K. Hyland and P. Shaw (Eds.), *The Routledge handbook of English for academic purposes* (pp. 361–375). London: Routledge.

Morley, L., Leonard, D., & David, M. (2002). Variations in Vivas: Quality and equality in British PhD assessments. *Studies in Higher Education, 27*(3): 263–273.

Morley, L., Leonard, D., & David, M. (2003). Quality and equality in British PhD assessment. *Quality Assurance in Education, 11*(2): 64–72.

NDPH Student Blog. (2017). *40 practice questions for viva preparation*. https://ndphblog.wordpress.com/2017/05/09/40-practice-questions-for-viva-preparation/.

Phillips, E., & Pugh, D. S. (2010). *How to get a PhD a handbook for students and their supervisors*. Maidenhead: Open University Press.

Pittman, C., & Karle, E. (2015). *Rewire your anxious brain: How to use the Neuroscience of Fear to end anxiety, panic, and worry*. Oakland, CA: New Harbinger Publications.

Regal, B. (2016). *PhD defenses around the world: A defense in Modern History and Literature from the USA*. https://www.evalantsoght.com/2016/12/phd-defenses-around-the-world-a-defense-in-modern-history-and-literature-from-the-usa.html

Saul, J. (2013). Implicit bias, stereotype threat, and women in philosophy. *Women in Philosophy*. https://oxford.universitypressscholarship.com/view/10.1093/acprof:oso/9780199325603.001.0001/acprof-9780199325603-chapter-3

Schwabisch, J. (2016). *Better presentations: A guide for scholars, researchers, and wonks*. New York: Columbia University Press.

Shields, P. (2018). *PhD defenses around the world: A defense from the University of Charleston*. https://www.evalantsoght.com/2018/08/phd-defenses-around-the-world-a-defense-from-the-university-of-charleston.html

Shimabukuro, K. (2018). *PhD defenses around the world: A defense from Literature at the University of New Mexico*. https://www.evalantsoght.com/2018/02/phd-defenses-around-the-world-a-defense-from-literature-at-the-university-of-new-mexico.html

Stanley, L., & Wise, S. (1993). *Breaking out again: Feminist ontology & epistemology*. London: Routledge.

Tinkler, P., & Jackson, C. (2000). Examining the doctorate: Institutional policy and the PhD examination process in Britain. *Studies in Higher Education, 25*(2): 167–180.

Trueman, C. (2018). *PhD defenses around the world: A defense in Northern Ireland*. https://www.evalantsoght.com/2018/02/phd-defenses-around-the-world-a-defense-in-northern-ireland.html

TU Delft. (2014). *Doctoral Regulations 2014*. 36.

Tufte, E. (1990). *Envision information*. Cheshire, CT: Graphics Pr.

Tufte, E. (1997). *Visual explanations: Images and quantities, evidence and narrative*. Cheshire, CT: Graphics Pr.

Tufte, E. (2001). *The visual display of quantitative information*. Cheshire, CT: Graphics Pr.

Tufte, E. (2006). *Beautiful evidence*. Cheshire, CT: Graphics Pr.

University of Leicester. (2020). *Practice viva questions*. https://www2.le.ac.uk/departments/doctoralcollege/training/eresources/study-guides/viva/prepare/questions

Vaccari, D., & Thangam, S. (2010). A proposed doctoral assessment procedure and rubric for science and engineering. 2010 Annual conference & exposition of the American Society for Engineering Education, Louisville, Kentucky.

van Vliet, A. (2017). *PhD defenses around the world: The textbook pantomime villain? An external examiner's view*. https://www.evalantsoght.com/2017/11/phd-defenses-around-the-world-the-textbook-pantomine-villain-an-external-examiners-view.html

Watts, J. H. (2012). Preparing doctoral candidates for the viva: Issues for students and supervisors. *Journal of Further and Higher Education, 36*(3): 371–381.

Wellington, J. (2010). Supporting students' preparation for the viva: Their pre-conceptions and implications for practice. *Teaching in Higher Education, 15*(1): 71–84.

Westerbeck, Z. D. (2020). *You are not alone: The only book you'll ever need to overcome anxiety and depression*. Costa Mesa, CA: Westerbeck Speaking and Coaching, Inc.

Yahaghi, H., Sorooshian, S., & Yahaghi, J. (2017). Viva delay. *Science and Engineering Ethics, 23*(3): 945–946.

5 Defences around the world

Introduction

This chapter is based on the more than 40 (and counting) testimonies from PhD students around the world about the format of their PhD defence and their experience, as well as references from the literature. While the world map of defences is not complete, the geographical breadth of the stories does give an idea of the differences and similarities in procedures worldwide, see Table 5.1, which uses the building blocks identified in Chapter 2. If you are interested in reading the full stories, you can find them on my (Eva's) blog PhD Talk under the "PhD defences around the world" title. I've also provided references to the individual posts for your convenience. The resulting overview is not complete, with some large countries such as India and China missing, but we hope that this chapter will give you an insight into the variety of defence formats that exists. We've organized this chapter by addressing each country separately. The order of countries is roughly by region, and you will observe that some geographical areas have commonalities in their defence formats, but

DOI: 10.4324/9780429347900-5

Table 5.1 Characterization of defence formats. B/A refers to defending the thesis before or after the finalization of the thesis. W/O refers to written or oral defence. Pu/Pr refers to public or private defence, 1/2 refers to single-step or double-step defence. F/C refers to fixed schedule or committee-driven schedule

Country	Name	B/A	W/O	Pu/Pr	1/2	F/C	Observations
Netherlands	Defence	A	O	Pu	1	F	Large committee, use of caps and gowns, beadle leads ceremony
Belgium	Defence	B/A	O	Pr/Pu	2	C	First, a private defence similar to the UK *viva*, then a celebratory public defence.
France	Defence	A	O	Pu*	1	C	Pu*: open to colleagues (lab members), but not friends and family
Germany	Defence	B	O	Pu	1	F	Notable variations among universities
Portugal	Defence	A	O	Pu	1	C	No formal dress code, defences tend to be long
Spain	Defence	A	O	Pu	1	C	Requirements to defend are part of the Spanish law.
Sweden	Defence	A	O	Pu	1	C	The committee evaluates and approves the thesis for defence. The opponent examines the candidate during the defence. Candidates receive ring and hat or laurel wreath before commencement.

Defences around the world 117

Finland	Disputas	A	O	Pu	1	F	Interaction between disputant (PhD candidate) and opponent. Candidates receive doctoral hat and sword before commencement.
Norway	Defence	A	O	Pu	1	F	Includes trial lecture by candidate
Bulgaria	Defence		O		1		Limited information available
Ukraine	Defence		O		1		Limited information available
Russia	*Viva*	A	O	Pr/Pu	2	C/F	The private defence is committee-driven and the public defence has a fixed time.
Georgia	Scientific debate	A	O		1		Limited information available
United Kingdom and Ireland	*Viva*	B	O	Pr	1	C	Variations of committee: only internal and external examiner, or with a Chair, and/or with the supervisor present.
United States	Defence	B	O/W	Pu/Pr	1/2	C	Many variations possible
Canada	*Viva*	B	O	Pu/Pr	1	C/F	Length of defence depends on university
Chile	Defence	A	O	Pu/Pr	2	C	Two-step defence
Australia	–	B	W	–	–	–	Written defence (traditionally)
New Zealand	*Viva*	B	O	Pr	1	C	Very similar to the UK
Japan	*Viva*	B	O	Pu	1	C	
Iran	*Viva*	B	O	Pu	1	C	Similar to USA
Pakistan	*Viva*	B	O	Pu	1	C	Similar to USA
Egypt	Defence	A	O	Pu	1	C	
South Africa	–	B	W	–	–	–	Written defence (traditionally)

there are also differences that mean we don't attempt any more subtle groupings of countries per continent.

The Netherlands

In the Netherlands, PhD defences are formal events (Hut, 2016; Lantsoght, 2011b; Muqoz Llancao, 2016). The thesis is finalized and printed before you defend. The defence starts with a 20 minute presentation for friends and family (without the committee), called the "lekenpraatje". The actual defence starts with the beadle, who is responsible for ensuring the protocol is followed, leading committee members to their seats. The *rector magnificus* (or their stand-in) opens the defence using the gavel. The beadle then asks the PhD candidate and two paranymphs[1] (helpers who sit next to the PhD candidate and who can assist, for example, in reading propositions[2]) to come up to the front. Then, the actual defence starts: the external committee members ask their questions first, and the promotor goes last. Even though the defence is held in English, the official language for addressing the PhD candidate ("*waarde promovenda*") and members of the committee is Dutch. For each question, the committee member asking it wears an academic cap. After exactly one hour, the beadle marks the end by saying "*hora est*" and beats the ceremonial staff on the floor. The beadle and committee retreat to a separate room to deliberate and sign the diploma. When the committee returns, the promotor hands over the diploma to the new doctor and gives a *laudatio* (congratulatory speech). Afterwards, there is a reception for all attendees, often followed by a dinner that evening.

Belgium

In Belgium (Debecker, 2016; Masuzzo, 2017) you have two defences: a closed and a public defence. The committee gives comments on your thesis and then you have a closed defence with your committee (without your supervisor(s) at Ghent University (Masuzzo, 2017), and with your supervisor and a Chair at Université Catolique de Louvain (Debecker, 2016)). The closed defence starts with a five minute introduction (Ghent) or 20 minute presentation on the research (UCL), and then the committee asks questions, sometimes chapter by chapter. At UCL, the time limit is three hours, but defences often go over time. The outcome of the closed defence is either: (1) defend again in a closed defence in a few months' time; (2) major revisions: send a new manuscript after three months and then see if the candidate can defend publicly; (3) minor revisions, which the committee won't check, and permission to defend publicly.

The next step is a public defence. The thesis is printed and final before the public defence. The committee dresses in caps and gowns. You present your work (40–45 minutes), and then the committee asks questions that are more focused on the broader scope of your work (10–15 minutes per committee member). The audience can ask questions as well. The public defence lasts about two hours. After the defence, the committee retreats and upon return they give the proclamation. A ceremonial aspect in Ghent is that the supervisor places the university hat on the head of the newly minted doctor. At UCL, the new doctor signs the diploma, which then goes to the rector for the final signature, and then the promotor gives a speech.

France

In France (Veronique, 2017) the committee consists of researchers from the same lab and university as the candidate, as well as external committee members. There are no formal rules for the defence. The audience of the defence includes all lab members but no family or friends. The defence starts with a presentation of about 30 minutes. Then, the actual defence takes place: the committee members ask their questions and provide their criticism of the work. After deliberation, the committee proclaims the acceptance of the thesis (sometimes with honors). Afterwards, it is time to celebrate the successful defence.

Germany

In Germany (Okonechnikov, 2017), the requirements for the defence vary between universities. The thesis is examined by the promotor, daily supervisor, and an external examiner – these examiners do not form part of the committee. The committee is made up of professors from your university. The day before the defence, you can read the examiners' evaluation and prepare for possible questions from the committee. The defence is public and has two parts: (1) a basic overview of your research area starting from theory (20 minutes) and (2) a detailed focus on a particular problem (10 minutes). During both steps, you get questions from the committee and the audience. After the defence, the thesis becomes available online.

Portugal

In Portugal (Abambres, 2019; Vreede, 2016), defences are rather informal: there is no dress code, and no locked doors, and it is expected that you will pass your defence. Defences can be long (up to three hours): 20 minutes for your presentation, 45 minutes for each of the two external committee members, and 30 minutes for each of the two local committee members. After the defence, the committee retires. When they return, they announce that "the candidate is now a doctor", which marks the end of the defence.

Spain

In Spain (Fariñas, 2017), between finishing your thesis and defending your thesis there is a fair amount of paperwork, complicated by the many changes to the laws regarding PhD requirements. The law prescribes that *"in the evaluation process and prior to the defence/viva, the university should guarantee advertising the final doctoral thesis so that other doctors can submit comments on the contents"* (Royal Decree 1393/2007, September 29th art. 21. 4 in de-Miguel, 2010). Once the thesis is approved by the supervisor, the doctoral committee appoints a defence committee (panel of examiners) based on the suggestions of the supervisor. At least two external experts need to give written feedback before the defence. The defence itself (Fariñas, 2017) is public. You first give a presentation, and then there is time for questions from the committee. After deliberation, you hear the outcome of your defence.

Sweden

In Sweden (Anonymous, 2016; Lund University, 2019), the committee approves the thesis before the defence. The committee consists of three professors, usually with one from another university. The thesis is thus submitted before the defence. The defence is held in a regular lecture room. There is no formal dress code, but most candidates opt for a suit. There's no time limit, and defences can last up to four hours (Anonymous, 2016). The peculiarity here is that the main actor during the defence is the *opponent*, who has not commented on the thesis before the defence and is not considered part of the committee (Kyvik, 2014). The opponent presents the thesis and examines the candidate (van der Ploeg, 2011). Nowadays, sometimes the candidate presents the thesis. In addition, there are questions from the committee members and the public but the actual defence is the interaction with the opponent. These questions are based on the thesis as well as your field of study. The only possible outcome from the opponent is pass or fail. The committee then retreats for deliberation and returns afterwards with the decision (pass or fail). Failing the defence is rare as the thesis is already approved by the committee (but not by the opponent) and considered final.

The official Latin diploma arrives after about three months, accompanied by a golden ring (you are married to the scientific method) inscribed with the date of the defence and your faculty, and either a tall hat with the emblem of the faculty (in science) or sometimes a laurel wreath (in humanities). The commencement ceremony (in Latin) is held once a year at the end of May, often in a cathedral. The dress code is evening wear. Outside the cathedral, cannons are fired.

Finland

In Finland (Mikhailova, 2016), you receive feedback on your dissertation from two external reviewers. They need to approve the thesis before you can defend. The defence is public, and usually attended by friends, family, colleagues, and collaborators. There are many old-fashioned formalities: a strict dress code and set phrases at the beginning and end of the defence. The committee consists of the disputant (PhD candidate), the opponent, and the custos (a professor from your institute, preferably but not necessarily the supervisor). They enter at exactly 12:15 pm. The audience stands while the committee walks to the front of the room. The custos opens the defence by briefly introducing the disputant and opponent. The disputant gives the *lectio praecursoria*: a general overview of the aims and background of the study. This presentation is followed by general remarks from the opponent (5 minutes). This is followed by the actual discussion (1–2 hours) between disputant and opponent. After this, the opponent stands up to give a statement about the overall quality of the thesis and the defence. The disputant thanks the opponent for the discussion and asks the audience for comments or questions. This is a formality – it is uncommon for the audience to actually ask questions. The custos closes the defence, opponent and disputant leave the room, and then the audience can leave as well. You receive a doctoral hat and doctoral sword after your defence, during the official commencement ceremony in May (University of Oulu, 2013).

Norway

In Norway (Kyvik, 2014), a committee of three members, with at least one international member, approves the thesis before the defence in a jointly written report. The defence is public and starts with a presentation of the candidate. Then, two of the committee members (often also called *opponents*) examine the candidate for about an hour. The audience can also ask questions but that is not common. Besides the defence, the candidate also has to give a public trial lecture on a topic other than the thesis, with two weeks' notice to prepare (Driggers, 2015). The purpose of this lecture is to test if the candidate can acquire knowledge on another topic than the thesis and share this knowledge in the style of a lecture. The committee also evaluates this lecture. After the defence and trial lecture, the committee writes a joint statement to confirm that the candidate has successfully passed.

Bulgaria

In Bulgaria (Petkova, 2011) you defend your thesis before a committee with five members, all of whom need to be associate or full professors. Within this committee, two reviewers are appointed who will take a leading role in the assessment of the PhD thesis and defence. All committee members evaluate the thesis. Important requirements are that the original contribution has to be clear and that 70%

of the thesis work should already be published. Following these procedures and the defence, you get your doctoral degree.

Ukraine

In Ukraine (Chekina, 2017), the committee members are all doctors with many years of experience (with many members often well past retirement age). You give your presentation and then receive questions from the committee. Your supervisor can assist in answering the questions and clarifying elements for the committee. Most questions will come from the main examiner, the *opponent*. After the defence, all committee members vote on the outcome of the defence. Nine months later, you receive your diploma.

Russia

In Russia (Gurevich & Yushuk, 2011; Voronina, 2017) the defence has two parts: a trial *viva* and a *viva*. The trial *viva* has a committee with an internal and external examiner. The external examiner can be from a different department or from another university. The trial *viva* is closed and the examiners ask detailed questions about the thesis. The goal of this defence is to evaluate the thesis and give feedback on how to improve it. After passing the trial *viva*, you get permission to defend your dissertation. Your thesis is first evaluated by the dissertational defence board. They then identify who from the dissertational defence board can serve on the committee. This committee writes a conclusion about the thesis for the dissertational defence board. When this conclusion is positive, the defence board accepts the thesis for defence, and appoints the official opponents and the Chair of the defence committee. The opponents send their evaluation of the thesis about two weeks before the defence so that you can prepare and address their comments.

The *viva* is public and takes two hours. It's common for friends, family, colleagues, and collaborators to attend. The head of the dissertational defence board opens the defence and the scientist secretary confirms that all documents have been received from the candidate. You then give a short presentation. During the defence, all members of the dissertational defence board can ask questions. This is followed by a short speech from the promotor. The scientist secretary then reads the conclusion of the organization where the research was carried out, that organization's review, and reviews on the extended abstract of the dissertation from all dissertational defence board members. You have to address these comments. The official opponents then read their feedback and you reply to these questions. Then, the members of the dissertational defence board discuss the thesis and, finally, you get to give a short speech to thank everyone. At the end, the dissertational defence board votes (in private) on the thesis – you need a two thirds majority voting in your favor to pass. After you receive a positive outcome, the dissertation defence board votes publicly on its draft conclusion and then closes the defence.

Georgia

The doctoral defence procedures in Georgia are influenced by those from Russia. The defence in Georgia (Pitskhelauri, Chikhladze, & Tsiskaridze, 2011) is public and should be advertised at least two weeks in advance. An additional requirement in Georgia is that your main contribution should already be published or accepted for publication in a peer-reviewed journal with impact factor. The committee which evaluates the written thesis includes independent experts from other universities without connection to your institution. This committee will then examine you during the defence.

The defence starts with a presentation, followed by the actual defence (described as the scientific debate), and ends with the conclusions of the dissertation committee. The thesis itself is assessed with a pass-fail grade and the final grade you receive for your doctoral degree follows a grading system going from *summa cum laude* (91%–100%) all the way down to *rite* (51%–60%). If you fail the thesis, you will have a chance to rewrite and present it again for evaluation and possible defence.

United Kingdom and Ireland

The *viva voce* in the United Kingdom and Ireland is different from the defence formats in continental Europe and has been analyzed and discussed more in the literature.

In the UK (Atkinson, 2016; Bodewits, 2018; Edwards, 2017; Imtiaz, 2016; Lantsoght, 2019; Trueman, 2018), the *viva* takes place behind closed doors. At some institutions (Dyer Saxon, 2016), there's also a transfer *viva* after the first year of the doctoral program, during which you defend your proposal to two internal examiners. During the actual *viva* at the end of your degree, the only people allowed to be there are you, your external examiner, your internal examiner, and, depending on the rules of your department, your supervisor and a Chair (Dyer

Saxon, 2016; Trueman, 2018). Usually, the *viva* starts with the internal examiner (or Chair, if present) explaining the procedures, followed by the external examiner asking you to summarize your research. Then, the committee gets to ask questions. In some cases (Bodewits, 2018; Imtiaz, 2016; Lantsoght, 2019), the examiners go page by page through the thesis. In other cases (Atkinson, 2016; Trueman, 2018), the examiners start with easy questions about the research in general and gradually move to more difficult questions (Dyer Saxon, 2016). There's no maximum length to the defence, with extreme cases lasting up to five hours (Edwards, 2017). Remenyi, Money, Price, and Bannister (2003) say: *"examiners sometimes, if not often, feel that they need to ask the candidate to add something to the dissertation so that the examiner has made a contribution to or just made their mark on the work".*

After the questioning, you leave the room to let the examiners deliberate. The possible outcome of this deliberation is fail, revise and resubmit, major corrections, minor corrections, or pass without corrections. If you fail, there is the possibility of being awarded an MPhil instead. However, failure is very rare as you would not be cleared to defend if there are major problems with your work – but it can happen in cases of academic fraud (Edwards, 2017). When you return to the room to hear your result, you receive feedback and a list of amendments to make if you have to make corrections. For minor corrections, you get three months and then the thesis is reviewed by the internal examiner, who will provide final approval of it. It often takes less time, and Imtiaz (2016) writes that it took him only ten days.

In terms of how the defence in the UK has changed over the last decade, Clarke (2013) observes that the defence may have become fairer and more consistent since the introduction of independent Chairs, recording of defences, and changes in the ways in which the reports of the committee members are used and made available to candidates.

After submitting a hard bound copy of the thesis to the library and a digital copy to the repository, you receive your degree in an official ceremony. You get to shake hands with the Chancellor of the university. All academics wear caps and gowns and the new doctors wear the academic dress that corresponds to the degree just obtained. Local officials also attend in official dress.

United States

In the United States, a variety of defence formats are used (Ames, 2016; Bartos, 2017; Lantsoght, 2011a; Newton, 2016) – and in exceptional cases, there is no oral defence (Berg, 2017). The committee usually consists of three or more faculty members from the institution itself (Shimabukuro, 2018), sometimes with an external committee member (Ames, 2016), and sometimes with a Chair. In the testimonies I (Eva) collected, the largest committee had six professors (Corcoran, 2018). Sometimes you will only know the identity of the final member of your committee a day prior to the defence (Lee, 2018). You can have a substitute member on call, in case of a last-minute emergency (Ames, 2016). In some cases, a committee member can join by telephone (Regal, 2016) or videoconference (Shimabukuro, 2018) and sometimes the entire defence is virtual (Shields, 2018).[3]

Some universities require a written permission to defend your thesis (Ames, 2016) and expect you to submit your thesis three weeks before the defence to your committee. In other cases, the committee may decide to postpone your defence when they feel the thesis is not ready yet to be defended (Killen, 2017). A particular dress code for the defence may not be required, but some candidates do mention that they dressed up for the occasion (and polished their shoes) (Regal, 2016).

The defence is usually public (Abboud, 2018; Bartos, 2017; Killen, 2017), at least in part, and sometimes it's available through livestreaming (Bartos, 2017; Shields, 2018). While private-only defences are not the norm in the United States, some universities consider defences as technically public but do not advertise them, so that in practice, the defence is private with only you and the committee present (Mallinson, 2016). Another possible format is the combination of two defences: a private defence with your committee only (Shields, 2018) and three weeks later, if all goes well, the public defence.

The procedures start with the opening presentation (a long presentation with slides) or statement (a short summary of your work), after which the Q&A starts, with or without an audience (Newton, 2016). The Q&A part depends on the university. In some cases, there are time limits for each committee member, for example 10–15 minutes for the second and third reader of the thesis (Newton, 2016). Other institutions have an overall time limit for the defence, for example two hours (Killen, 2017) including the deliberation after the defence. At some institutions, only the committee members ask questions, but in other cases the audience can ask questions as well (Shields, 2018). You can mostly expect questions about your methodology, the broader field of research, and the arguments used to support your hypothesis, or the main ideas of the thesis – for example how you define certain aspects, and why you did X rather than Y (Shimabukuro,

2018). Sometimes, you will also be required to do a form of analysis on the spot (Abboud, 2018). The Chair can make a contribution at the end of the defence to place the work in the broader field of research (Newton, 2016).

After the defence, the committee deliberates on the outcome. When you and your audience return to the room, you are congratulated on your achievement. When the defence is held through videoconferencing, you will close the online meeting room and wait for a call from your Chair or supervisor (Shields, 2018). You then receive suggestions for improving your thesis which you will finalize in the weeks after the defence. The final ceremony is the formal commencement ceremony.

For the rare case where there is no oral defence (Berg, 2017), there is a final seminar in which you present the work you have done. There's no defence before the committee – all that needs to be done is to get the signature of each committee member and you are ready to graduate. The one-on-one meetings you have with the committee members can feel like mini-defences.

Canada

In Canada, defence formats are influenced by those of both the United Kingdom and the United States – and formats differ across universities. Committees in Canada tend to be on the larger side, including internal members, a member from a different department, an external member, your supervisor, and the Chair of the committee (who has no voting rights in the deliberation) (Gill, 2017; Jacobs, 2018). In some cases, teleconferencing is used for the participation of the external member. The defence sometimes starts with a seminar (45 minutes) to summarize your research. All graduate students may be required to attend these seminars, as well as the committee (Gill, 2017). After the seminar, the defence continues in a smaller conference room – just you and the committee. There are two rounds of questions in the defence. During the first round, every committee member gets a maximum of 20 minutes to ask questions. During the second round, the committee members get extra time to address anything they would like – this round is more like a conversation between you and your committee. After each member of the committee declares they have no further questions you have to leave the room and the committee deliberates. The outcome of the deliberation is similar to that in the UK and, often, (minor) corrections are required before the thesis can be finalized. The Chair gives the decision, and congratulates you by calling you Doctor. At other institutions, your supervisor gives you the news in the hallway where you're waiting for the outcome of the deliberation. The official graduation ceremony is called a convocation, held once per semester.

Chile

In Chile (Muqoz Llancao, 2016), you have to pass at least two previous evaluations (mini-defences) from the PhD committee before you are allowed to defend your thesis. The private defence is a three to four hour-long grilling by the committee members. The last step is a public defence which friends and family can attend, with an hour-long presentation of the research after which the public can ask questions. After this step, the main supervisors congratulate the new doctor and present a small gift from the university. One year later, the university invites all new doctors to a formal ceremony, where they will each receive a medal (Universidad de Chile, 2019; Wikipedia, 2019).

Australia

Written defences are most common in Australia, although you may be required to give a presentation before the final submission of your thesis (Mežek & Swales, 2016). After you submit your thesis, it is sent to two anonymous external reviewers (Coupland, 2018), who treat your thesis as if it were a very long journal article (Golding, Sharmini, & Lazarovitch., 2014). The outcome of the review process is also similar to receiving reviews from a journal article, with a decision ranging from "Accepted as-is" to "Significant further work required for thesis to satisfy requirements of PhD". You are required to address the comments of the reviewers before the thesis can be accepted and published. And just as with a journal article, the acceptance comes with a rather unceremonious email saying that you just earned your PhD degree.

New Zealand

In New Zealand (Bright, 2016; Murugayah, 2019), the PhD defence is similar to (but not exactly the same as) the defence in the UK. Some universities require a departmental seminar before your defence (Murugayah, 2019), which can be open to the public. The committee consists of the convenor (the Chair), three examiners, and the supervisors. The examiners can attend in person or via videoconference. The supervisor does not participate in the defence. You receive the (anonymous) reports of the examiners a few days before the defence so that you can prepare. The time between submitting your thesis and receiving the reports is on average three months, but can be up to a year (Murugayah, 2019).

The defence itself is private. You start the defence by giving an overview of your research, which can be rather brief (five (Bright, 2016) to ten (Murugayah, 2019) minutes). After this, the questioning starts. You can guess the likely topics of these questions from the written reports of the examiners. The defence can be structured around the main areas of your research, such as methods, process, and findings, and discuss links with other research in the field and future research (Bright, 2016). Another format for the defence is to go through the thesis page by page (Murugayah, 2019). After the questions, you and your supervisor leave the room so the committee can deliberate on the outcome of the defence. The possible outcomes are the same as in the UK. After the deliberation, the convener calls you and your supervisor back in, and if all went well, the convener congratulates you. The degree is officially conferred during a commencement ceremony.

Japan

In Japan (Koso, 2016), you either earn your PhD degree through a three-year graduate program that includes research and coursework ("*katei hakase*" or degree PhD), or by thesis alone ("*ronbun hakase*" or thesis PhD). For the degree PhD option, the system is similar to the USA: coursework, defending a proposal, and then the thesis and defence (the Japanese system does not have qualifying exams). For the defence, the committee consists of three reviewers: your supervisor, an internal examiner, and an external examiner. The defence itself is public. It consists of three parts: presentation, questions, and review. The presentation lasts 40 minutes and focuses on your main research findings and conclusions. Then come questions from the committee and the audience. The final part is the review, during which the committee members give their general impression of your work and their comments on how to improve it. The official confirmation that you have passed your defence comes weeks after the defence itself. The last step is submitting your thesis in hard copy, after which you can receive your degree. The official PhD degree awarding ceremonies are in March. If you finish later during the year, you go through a smaller ceremony.

Iran

In Iran, defences follow the format from the USA (Mežek & Swales, 2016) and are in the presence of an audience (Izadi, 2017). We do not have a full testimony from Iran, but interested readers can refer to Section on United States.

Pakistan

In Pakistan (Haque, 2011), very few universities currently offer the PhD degree. Where this degree is offered, the defence is public and tends to be influenced by practice in the USA.

Egypt

In Egypt (Hassan, 2018), there are quite some hurdles to overcome if you want to make it to the end of the PhD. Before you can defend your thesis, you need all your supervisors to agree on the final version. It can be tricky when they have conflicting opinions. When the thesis is accepted, you are cleared to defend. The defence is very formal, with a formal dress code. The defence starts with a presentation of 45 minutes to an hour. After the presentation, your committee asks questions about your work. An important aspect during the PhD defence in Egypt is your catering – you are expected to bring snacks for the committee and bring lunch for after the defence. After the defence, all committee members sign, and a few months later, you will receive your PhD diploma.

Notes

1 In the Netherlands, paranymphs are assistants of the doctoral candidate who is defending. They sit by your side and can only be called upon to read excerpts from your thesis out loud – they don't actually get to help you answer questions.
2 In the Netherlands, you defend your thesis and propositions. The propositions are a number of statements, some from your research, some general ones from your field, and some from outside your field, which you should be able to argue for during your defence.
3 WebEx, Zoom, Teams, GoToMeeting, Jitsi, Skype, Skype for Business ... We've all used and gained experience with many videoconferencing tools in 2020.

References

Abambres, M. (2019). *PhD defenses around the world: A defense in Portugal*. https://www.evalantsoght.com/2019/03/phd-defenses-around-the-world-a-defense-in-portugal.html

Abboud, V. (2018). *PhD defenses around the world: A defense at Wayne State University*. https://www.evalantsoght.com/2018/10/phd-defenses-around-the-world-a-defense-at-wayne-state-university.html

Ames, R. (2016). *PhD defenses around the world: A defense in medicine from New York*. https://www.evalantsoght.com/2016/06/phd-defenses-around-the-world-a-defense-in-medicine-from-new-york.html

Anonymous. (2016). *PhD defenses around the world: A defense in Sweden*. https://www.evalantsoght.com/2016/04/phd-defenses-around-the-world-a-defense-in-sweden.html

Atkinson, K. (2016). *PhD defenses around the world: A Viva in the United Kingdom*. https://www.evalantsoght.com/2016/05/phd-defenses-around-the-world-a-viva-in-the-united-kingdom.html

Bartos, S. (2017). *PhD defenses around the world: A defense in nursing from the United States*. https://www.evalantsoght.com/2017/10/phd-defenses-around-the-world-a-defense-in-nursing-from-the-united-states.html

Berg, M. (2017). *PhD defenses around the world: A defense (without a defense) in biology from UC Berkeley*. https://www.evalantsoght.com/2017/10/phd-defenses-around-the-world-a-defense-without-a-defense-in-biology-from-uc-berkeley.html

Bodewits, K. (2018). *PhD defenses around the world: A defense in chemistry at the University of Edinburgh*. https://www.evalantsoght.com/2018/09/phd-defenses-around-the-world-a-defense-in-chemistry-at-the-university-of-edinburgh.html

Bright, F. (2016). *PhD defenses around the world: A Viva in New Zealand*. https://www.evalantsoght.com/2016/09/phd-defenses-around-the-world-a-viva-in-new-zealand.html

Chekina, V. (2017). *PhD defenses around the world: A defense from Ukraine*. https://www.evalantsoght.com/2017/09/phd-defenses-around-the-world-a-defense-from-ukraine.html

Clarke, G. (2013). Developments in doctoral assessment in the UK. In M. Kompf & P. M. Denicolo (Eds.), *Critical issues in higher education* (pp. 23–36). Rotterdam: Sense Publisheres.

Corcoran, V. (2018). *PhD defenses around the world: A defense in medieval history at The Catholic University of America.* https://www.evalantsoght.com/2018/09/phd-defenses-around-the-world-a-defense-in-medieval-history-at-the-catholic-university-of-america.html

Coupland, K. (2018). *PhD defenses around the world: A defense in neuroscience from Australia.* https://www.evalantsoght.com/2018/02/phd-defenses-around-the-world-a-defense-in-neuroscience-from-australia.html

de-Miguel, M. (2010). The evaluation of doctoral thesis. A model proposal. *RELIEVE: Revista Electrónica de Investigación y Evaluación Educativa, 16*(1), 1–17.

Debecker, D. (2016). *PhD defenses around the world: A defense in Belgium.* https://www.evalantsoght.com/2016/05/phd-defenses-around-the-world-a-defense-in-belgium.html

Driggers, R. (2015). Norwegian doctoral defence: Editorial. *Applied Optics, 54*(19), ED7–ED8, doi:10.1364/AO.54.000ED7.

Dyer Saxon, E. (2016). *PhD defenses around the world: A PhD viva from Trinity College, Dublin, Ireland.* https://www.evalantsoght.com/2016/08/phd-defenses-around-the-world-a-phd-viva-from-trinity-college-dublin-ireland.html

Edwards, A. (2017). *PhD defenses around the world: A viva in linguistics at Cambridge.* https://www.evalantsoght.com/2017/05/phd-defenses-around-the-world-a-viva-in-linguistics-at-cambridge.html

Fariñas, L. (2017). *PhD defenses around the world: A defense in Spain.* https://www.evalantsoght.com/2017/01/phd-defenses-around-the-world-a-defense-in-spain.html

Gill, M. (2017). *PhD defenses around the world: A defense in Chemistry from Canada.* https://www.evalantsoght.com/2017/06/phd-defenses-around-the-world-a-defense-in-chemistry-from-canada.html

Golding, C., Sharmini, S., & Lazarovitch, A. (2014). What examiners do: What thesis students should know. *Assessment & Evaluation in Higher Education, 39*(5), 563–576. doi:10.1080/02602938.2013.859230.

Gurevich, K. G., & Yushuk, N. D. (2011). System of research staff training in Russian federation. *Turkish Journal of Biochemistry, 36*(1), 31–34.

Haque, A. (2011). Current status of PhD education in biomedicine and health sciences in Pakistan. *Turkish Journal of Biochemistry, 36*(1), 42–44.

Hassan, M. (2018). *PhD defenses around the world: A PhD defense in Egypt.* https://www.evalantsoght.com/2018/10/phd-defenses-around-the-world-a-phd-defense-in-egypt.html

Hut, R. (2016). *PhD defenses around the world: Tinkering at a defense in Delft.* https://www.evalantsoght.com/2016/09/phd-defenses-around-the-world-tinkering-at-a-defense-in-delft.html

Imtiaz, S. A. (2016). *PhD defenses around the world: A viva at Imperial College.* https://www.evalantsoght.com/2016/04/phd-defenses-around-the-world-a-viva-at-imperial-college.html

Izadi, A. (2017). Culture-generality and culture-specificity of face: Insights from argumentative talk in Iranian dissertation defences. *Pragmatics and Society, 8*(2), 208–230. doi:10.1075/ps.8.2.03iza.

Jacobs, S. (2018). *PhD defenses around the world: I passed and you will too.* https://www.evalantsoght.com/2018/12/phd-defenses-around-the-world-i-passed-and-you-will-too.html

Killen, M. (2017). *PhD defenses around the world: A defense in Education in the USA.* https://www.evalantsoght.com/2017/12/phd-defenses-around-the-world-a-defense-in-education-in-the-usa.html

Koso, A. (2016). *PhD defenses around the world: A defense in Japan.* https://www.evalantsoght.com/2016/09/phd-defenses-around-the-world-a-defense-in-japan.html

Kyvik, S. (2014). Assessment procedures of Norwegian PhD theses as viewed by examiners from the USA, the UK and Sweden. *Assessment & Evaluation in Higher Education, 39*(2), 140–153. doi:10.1080/02602938.2013.798395.

Lantsoght, E. (2011a). *A PhD defense at Georgia Tech.* https://www.evalantsoght.com/2011/08/a-phd-defense-at-georgia-tech.html

Lantsoght, E. (2011b). *A PhD defense at TU Delft.* https://www.evalantsoght.com/2011/01/a-phd-defense-at-tu-delft.html

Lantsoght, E. (2019). *Advice for the PhD defense from examiners.* https://www.evalantsoght.com/2019/11/advice-for-the-phd-defense-from-examiners.html

Lee, C. (2018). *PhD defenses around the world: A defense at Ohio State.* https://www.evalantsoght.com/2018/08/phd-defenses-around-the-world-a-defense-at-ohio-state.html

Lund University. (2019). *The role of Swedish higher education.* https://www.lunduniversity.lu.se/about/about-lund-university/the-role-of-swedish-higher-education.

Mallinson, D. J. (2016). *PhD defenses around the world: A defense in political science from Penn State.* https://www.evalantsoght.com/2016/06/phd-defenses-around-the-world-a-defense-in-political-science-from-penn-state.html

Masuzzo, P. (2017). *PhD defenses around the world: A defense in Bioinformatics in Belgium.* https://www.evalantsoght.com/2017/06/phd-defenses-around-the-world-a-defense-in-bioinformatics-in-belgium.html

Mežek, Š., & Swales, J. M. (2016). PhD defences and vivas. In K. Hyland, & P. Shaw (Eds.), *The Routledge handbook of English for academic purposes* (pp. 361–375). London: Routledge.

Mikhailova, A. (2016). *PhD defenses around the world: A defense in Finland*. https://www.evalantsoght.com/2016/06/phd-defenses-around-the-world-a-defense-in-finland.html

Muqoz Llancao, P. (2016). *PhD defenses around the world: Universidad de Chile and University of Groningen, the Netherlands*. https://www.evalantsoght.com/2016/03/phd-defenses-around-the-world-universidad-de-chile-and-university-of-groningen-the-netherlands.html

Murugayah, S. A. (2019). *PhD defenses around the world: A PhD defense from New Zealand*. https://www.evalantsoght.com/2019/05/phd-defenses-around-the-world-a-phd-defense-from-new-zealand.html

Newton, R. (2016). *PhD defenses around the world: A defense in California*. https://www.evalantsoght.com/2016/04/phd-defenses-around-the-world-a-defense-in-california.html

Okonechnikov, K. (2017). *PhD defenses around the world: A defense in Germany*. https://www.evalantsoght.com/2017/10/phd-defenses-around-the-world-a-defense-in-germany.html

Petkova, D. (2011). PhD education in Bulgaria. *Turkish Journal of Biochemistry, 36*(1), 45–48.

Pitskhelauri, N., Chikhladze, N., & Tsiskaridze, A. (2011). New Paradigm of PhD education at Tbilisi State University Faculty of Medicine in Georgia. *Turkish Journal of Biochemistry, 36*(1), 82–86.

Regal, B. (2016). *PhD defenses around the world: A defense in modern history and literature from the USA*. https://www.evalantsoght.com/2016/12/phd-defenses-around-the-world-a-defense-in-modern-history-and-literature-from-the-usa.html

Remenyi, D., Money, A., Price, D., & Bannister, F. (2003). The doctoral viva: A great educational experience of a gun fight at the OK Corral? *Irish Journal of Management, 24*(2), 105–116.

Shields, P. (2018). *PhD defenses around the world: A defense from the University of Charleston*. https://www.evalantsoght.com/2018/08/phd-defenses-around-the-world-a-defense-from-the-university-of-charleston.html

Shimabukuro, K. (2018). *PhD defenses around the world: A defense from Literature at the University of New Mexico*. https://www.evalantsoght.com/2018/02/phd-defenses-around-the-world-a-defense-from-literature-at-the-university-of-new-mexico.html

Trueman, C. (2018). *PhD defenses around the world: A defense in Northern Ireland*. https://www.evalantsoght.com/2018/02/phd-defenses-around-the-world-a-defense-in-northern-ireland.html

Universidad de Chile. (2019). *Distinción Medalla Doctoral Universidad de Chile*. http://www.uchile.cl/portal/presentacion/simbolos/medallas-y-distinciones/7967/distincion-medalla-doctoral-universidad-de-chile. Accessed 15 November 2019.

University of Oulu. (2013). *The ninth conferment ceremony of the University of Oulu*. https://www.oulu.fi/confermentceremony/in_english

van der Ploeg, I. (2011). Quality assurance in doctoral education experiences from Karolinska Institutet. *Turkish Journal of Biochemistry, 36*(1), 67–68.

Veronique. (2017). *PhD defenses around the world: A defense in medicine from France*. https://www.evalantsoght.com/2017/04/phd-defenses-around-the-world-a-defense-in-medicine-from-france.html

Voronina, A. (2017). *PhD defesces around the world: A defense from Russia*. https://www.evalantsoght.com/2017/11/phd-defenses-around-the-world-a-defense-from-russia.html

Vreede, B. (2016). *PhD defenses around the world: PhD defense in Portugal*. https://www.evalantsoght.com/2016/03/phd-defenses-around-the-world-phd-defense-in-portugal.html

Wikipedia (2019). Doctoral ring. https://en.wikipedia.org/wiki/Doctoral_ring. Accessed 15/11/2019.

6 Your PhD defence

The big day

Introduction

Finally, it is the day of your PhD Defence – your Big Day – the culmination of years of effort, ups and downs, struggles and challenges, victories and exciting achievements. This is the day when you showcase your knowledge, your years of study and research. This is the day when you demonstrate that you can conduct an independent research study: after all, this is what a PhD is awarded for.

You might feel that you are expected to approach this day with confidence and excitement. In reality, you may feel anxiety, apprehension, fear of bombing it, fear of appearing stupid and not being able to answer questions, or fear of freezing with stage fright and failing it.

In my (Olga's) ten years of hearing stories from PhD students in my coaching there wasn't one single student who was not afraid of or worried about their imminent PhD defence. This included students who passed with flying colors, with no corrections(!), or with minor corrections. Those students worried about passing their PhD defence as much as any other student. If right now you are worried and it's paralyzing you and hindering your preparation, we want you to know that you are not alone. It is very common and very normal and this chapter will give you tools and strategies to prepare you best for your special day!

Our advice in this chapter includes how you can prepare yourself for the Big Day during the last few days before it, and what to do right before and during the defence day. For advice regarding the weeks of preparation before the defence, refer to Chapter 4. You will have advice from former PhD students and committee members. You will also learn from research insights about the dynamics of the defence day. We will discuss eating and resting well, knowing your itinerary for the day, and making sure you have all the materials you are required to bring or want to use during the defence. You will learn how you can show up for your Big Day mentally and emotionally prepared and with the right mindset.

Let's do it!

The last days before the defence

Preparation for your Big Day in the last days beforehand will include the practical preparation we discussed at length in Chapter 4. Here is the summary of scientific activities that you can focus on, if you have not already done so:

- Practice your presentation, by yourself, and in front of your friends, colleagues or supervisor.
- In particular, practice the timing of your presentation.

- Finish other last-minute preparations for your presentation, such as hand-outs, posters, or samples.
- Re-read your thesis (on how to re-read your thesis most productively, see the section "General preparation before the defence").
- Re-read key research papers and review articles.
- Read newly published articles in your research area.
- Read papers published by your committee members and papers on the topics of their research area.
- Prepare yourself for the committee's questions (see the section "How to prepare for committee questions").

Preparation for the PhD defence is not all about intellectual preparation, it also includes eating well, resting and getting yourself into the right state of mind. To be as fit as possible for your defence, make sure you take extra good care of yourself in the final days. Eat well and get enough sleep on those days. For the day of the defence itself, think about what to eat that won't upset your stomach while you're nervous and don't forget to take your water bottle for before and during your defence.

Go to your defence well-rested. It is not always possible to follow this advice, for example when you need to return to your university for your defence and are dealing with jetlag, or when you have small children. Relax during the afternoon and evening before the Big Day. If you know you usually toss and turn in bed before a big event, plan an afternoon and evening of relaxing activities. If it helps you, add in some physical exercise to tire your body. I (Eva) remember that the evening before my defence, I made sure I had everything ready and packed for the next day. I did a more extensive evening beauty routine, and then I read a novel in bed with my cat and my husband by my side while sipping a cup of herbal tea. And I actually slept well that night. In the testimonies I (Eva) collected on the PhD defence, there's also advice on resting beforehand. The night before the defence Trueman (2018) was told not to study, but instead to relax, be pampered, and try not to think about what was ahead. If you need to travel from abroad to defend your thesis because you've already left your institution, travel a few days early to get over any jetlag (Kamal, 2019).

The day of the defence

Make an itinerary for the day itself. Write down what you have to do and when, and leave plenty of time for every step. When your friends and family arrive, you want to have enough time to greet them, instead of having to run off to take care of something – plan accordingly.

Make a list of the material you need to take to your defence and prepare everything the day before. This material can include:

- your presentation on a flash drive,
- your dissertation,
- your laptop,
- extra copies of your dissertation for the audience (especially if the book has already been printed),
- blank sheets of paper so you can make notes during questions from the committee and for drawing sketches to support your replies to committee questions,
- a whiteboard marker if you're using a whiteboard, or chalk if you're using a blackboard, and
- any other visual material you want to show during the defence.

If friends are helping you out with smaller tasks, make sure you know where they have to be and at what time, and let them know. In addition, make sure your promotor, committee members, and others involved in your defence (paranymphs if you have them) know where they have to be and when. Better repeat once more to everybody involved where and when they have to be, than have to call somebody because you can't locate them. If you need some time alone right before your defence, tell a friend what you are going to do, so nobody gets worried about you disappearing. If you prefer relaxing through social interaction, then enjoy mingling with your friends and family.

Most importantly: enjoy the day of your defence. You have worked towards this day for years – the heavy lifting has been done. Everything else is just the icing on the cake. You are the expert on your research. If your defence is public, part of its function is celebratory – your friends and family are there to support you and then celebrate your achievement. Appreciate having your loved ones with you on this Big Day. An additional thought worth repeating to yourself, is that everybody wants to perform well in a defence[1] (regardless of whether it is public or private) (Mežek & Swales, 2016). The Chair wants to demonstrate leadership during the day. The committee members want to demonstrate their expert knowledge and at the same time show their humanity and professionalism. You want to proudly defend your research and display your original contribution to your field to everyone involved in the defence. Everybody wants to do well; nobody has the intention to sabotage the defence. Your committee members want you to pass this rite so that they can welcome you as a newly minted doctor in their ranks.

Special needs

If you are a special needs student, discuss with your supervisor in advance what you will need to be able to defend without barriers. Reach out to the right support offices within your university to make your necessary arrangements. Ask your supervisor to inform committee members about your condition, what they need to consider during the defence, and which additional tools may be necessary. If you are the first special needs student to graduate in your research group, you may find it more difficult to navigate the special needs issues in your defence. Don't suffer in silence but get the support you need to be able to shine without obstructions. Remember that in most countries, it is your legal right to get the support and accommodations you need.

Some advice for the defence day from former students

In the testimonies from former PhD students that I (Eva) collected, I found the following practical tips for the Big Day: if (part of) your committee and/or audience will be joining in by video- or teleconference, make sure you arrive in advance in the room to set up all the equipment and check and double check that everything is running smoothly (Shimabukuro, 2018). Book IT support if you are new to the hardware in the conference room. Check the room a few days before the defence to see what you need to bring. Make sure you don't forget the small things, such as the right cables to connect everything.

Some advice for the defence from committee members

Committee members want you to remember that there are countries where failing a PhD defence is very uncommon (such as the Netherlands). Similarly, the defence in the US should be just a formality – if it is more than that, your adviser has dropped the ball. If you get as far as your defence, that means your supervisor considers you ready. Therefore, the advice is generally not to worry about it; you will pass (Lantsoght, 2019).

Enjoy yourself, it's your day. Have fun. Remember that research is fun. The whole audience is there to support you. Even your committee members know that the defence is your day, and their questions are only there to make you shine even more as well as to foster a debate between academics: you and your committee. Van Vliet (2017) comments: *"It would be great if the candidate comes out of the viva with new knowledge and insights, in addition to the blood, sweat and tears!"*

Research insights

In terms of the assessment process itself, Watts (2012) mentions that in recent times it has become more common for committee members to inform students at the start of the *viva* about the outcome of their thesis submission. However, this practice is still relatively rare and most students can expect to have to engage with examiners' questions in defence of their work as part of the assessment process. Similarly, Ryder (2014) found that only 20.9% of the respondents in his survey about the *viva* in the UK were told at the beginning of their defence that they had passed.

Clarke (2013) pointed out that the assessment of the defence depends on two elements: the candidate's output (thesis, knowledge of the field, and ability to defend) and outcomes (personal skills and abilities). Some students will produce a strong thesis (output) but may be less adept at defending their position during the defence. Others might not excel at written or practical work but will prove during the defence that they have mastery of the field. When it comes to making the evaluation of doctoral students more uniform, we perhaps should accept a certain level of inconsistency – this may be inevitable given the nature of the doctorate and the variables involved, which change on each occasion:

- the candidate is different,
- the committee is different,
- each subject or field has particular expectations, and
- each candidate has their own strengths and weaknesses.

The way in which a committee weighs output and outcomes is variable.

To further explore the outcomes (sometimes referred to as the hidden elements of the defence), and the emotional aspects thereof, Trafford and Leshem (2002) observed and analyzed one UK-style *viva* in depth. They found that non-verbal communication plays an important role. Analyzing the defence and the perceptions of all involved, the authors propose that a defence can be explained by three sets of variables: explicit doctorateness in the thesis design, emotional and scholarly resilience, and the social dynamics of the *viva*. Doctorateness means scholarship, being a sound researcher; emotional and scholarly resilience means being emotionally strong under pressure, and the social dynamics are related to being able to read

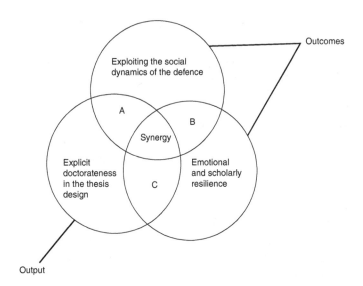

Figure 6.1 Domains of defence and the location of synergy (Trafford and Leshem 2002), including distinction made by Clarke (2013).

the social situation of the defence. The social context is important: for both the committee members and the candidate, the defence is a "rite of passage" unlike anything occurring in daily life.

Where social dynamics and doctorateness overlap, we find enthusiasm and excitement about the research (A in Figure 6.1). Where the social dynamics and emotional and scholarly resilience overlap, we find a willingness and ability to defend the "I Believe" factor of doctorateness in the thesis (B in Figure 6.1). Finally, where doctorateness and resilience overlap, we find confidence in the architecture, design, conduct and conceptual conclusions of the research (C in Figure 6.1). Where the three aspects overlap, we have synergy (see Figure 6.1). The authors offer the proposition that: *"the greater the extent of synergy between explicit scholarship, personal resilience, and interpersonal awareness of the candidate towards the process of the viva, the more likely it is that the thesis will be successfully defended".*

For the *viva* in the UK, Watts (2012) observes that there is no moderation of doctoral result, with no peer review or external examination as for taught undergraduate and postgraduate awards. There can be no appeal against the outcome by a student on the grounds of academic judgement, only on the basis of process. This suggests that the doctoral candidate, as "customer" in a developing market culture for education, may invoke their consumer rights to press for clearer criteria regarding outcomes and for visibility and transparency of process to ensure fairness and consistency. Fear of appeals and litigation associated with the "consumer" status of the student may have resulted in "cozy" arrangements between supervisor(s) and colleagues in other institutions to act as external committee members for each other, guaranteeing not to "rock the boat". One might wonder whether the defence, in the absence of rigor, has become a token formality with a consequent devaluation of the doctoral degree. A possible solution to this problem is opening up the UK-style *viva* to a larger and more diverse committee and/or to use a grading rubric to explain the outcome of the thesis and *viva* assessment to the student. However, we've seen in Chapter 2 that there is not much enthusiasm in the UK to move towards the format of the continental European defence.

Dealing with anxiety on the day of the defence

Understanding your anxiety

Your Big Day is here, and by now you have probably received good luck wishes and been told that you will do well. Yet, you might be feeling the opposite of knowledgeable and confident. You might in fact feel huge anxiety right before and on the day of your defence. In the section "Dealing with anxiety before the thesis defence", we have discussed those feelings in detail and here is a short summary of them. You might fear or be anxious that during your defence you will

- fail, or your presentation will go badly,
- not be able to answer committee questions,
- be judged by your colleagues or friends on how much you know and on your presentation skills,
- not be able to explain certain difficulties with your research or the challenges in interpretation of your results.

You may feel that you have not done enough, or you may feel anxious about a committee member with whom you have a difficult relationship, as we discussed in Chapter 4. Many PhD students say that this kind of anxiety is strongest right before the defence but interestingly it goes away as soon as the defence begins. It is as if the mind thinks: *"It is happening now and it is OK. I have not died"*. You stop worrying and start facing reality more constructively.

Strategies for dealing with anxiety on the day of the defence

In the section "Dealing with anxiety before the thesis defence" we discussed a number of strategies to help you deal with the fears and anxieties you might be feeling, and go through the day of your defence with confidence. Here is a brief summary of those strategies:

1. During your defence, focus on demonstrating that you have become an independent researcher – that is what the PhD degree is awarded for – and do not worry that your research is not so novel or not such a huge breakthrough.
2. Put aside your negative thoughts about not deserving the PhD degree and go into your defence with confidence, believing that you deserve the doctoral degree. Be ready to receive it.
3. Allow for a process of grieving and letting go of this period of your life as a PhD student and start embracing the next period of your life after the defence.

A further suggestion for dealing with anxiety is based on the premise that we humans can only predominantly experience one big feeling at a time. You can use that on the morning of your Big Day. Instead of ruminating on your negative thoughts, you can focus on a different, more positive feeling that will help you to feel better. My (Olga's) suggestion has always been to focus on gratitude: gratitude for everything good that happened during your PhD studies and gratitude to everyone who has put some time into helping you during all those years. Start remembering all the good things that happened to you: even if there were many difficulties and challenges, there were probably also many good, interesting, exciting, and fun moments. Remember all your achievements and accomplishments, and anything you have celebrated during the years of your PhD. Also think about the people who helped you during your PhD journey.

On the morning of his PhD defence one of my (Olga's) clients went around the department thanking his peers, mates and colleagues for helping him throughout his PhD and this is how he passed the time before his *viva*. Instead of feeling anxious, he focused on gratitude and managed to go into his PhD defence with a positive state of mind. Think about it this way: by actively focusing on gratitude, you will experience less anxiety, improve your mood, and go into your PhD defence with greater confidence.

Advice from former PhD students

In the testimonies of former PhD students, we find the following advice for dealing with anxiety on the day of the defence:

If you are nervous on the day of your defence, you can go for a run to release some of that nervous energy (Corcoran, 2018; Kamal, 2019). If you feel nervous, eat something light. Before the actual defence, you can listen to a song that inspires you to get in the right frame of mind (Corcoran, 2018). Kamal (2019) listened to her "focus song" to feel confident. In terms of framing the defence, you can see it as an opportunity to look back at what you have created and learned, and all the people that helped you get there (Ames, 2016).

If you are cleared to defend your thesis, there is a reason why you have made it thus far. You would not be allowed to defend if your supervisor did not feel confident that your work can stand the criticism of experts in the field. You've already almost made it. Remember that "*No one knows your research better than you do, you are the expert of your PhD*" (Trueman, 2018). You know your work best (Kamal, 2019). The advisor of Corcoran (2018) mentioned that the defence is your proverbial victory lap: both an endurance challenge and a celebration after years of hard work.

What I (Eva) read in many testimonies on the PhD defence is that there is always a moment when you start to feel more confident. Abboud (2018) calls this the moment when you know the experience is yours. You are at a point in the defence and start to realize that (1) you really are doing this, and (2) you can do this.

The more vocal members of your committee may start to drag you down a rabbit hole of ever more complex questions on a small detail of your work. At the same time, there are other people in your committee who may find this unnecessary and feel sympathy for you. Your supporters may not make themselves known (Jacobs, 2018), but they are present. Similarly, you will notice during the rest of your career that there are quiet, senior colleagues who will show acts of kindness that can be crucial in moving your career forward. Shimabukuro (2018) adds that

> no matter how the defence goes, how you feel, both in the ramp up and afterwards, as long as you pass, that is what matters. Once they say 'doctor' they're not going to take it back. The rest just becomes things to check off the list.

Finally, your PhD defence is not a defining moment in your life. It's the pinnacle of years of work, but there are far more important things in life (Jacobs, 2018). If you want to place things in context, read the testimony of Mallinson (2016) – his first child was expected on almost the same day as his defence. In the broader scope of things, becoming a parent certainly trumps answering the questions of your committee. He wrote of this experience:

> The wonder of his birth certainly overshadowed the fact that I had reached a culminating point in my educational journey. And therein lies the greatest lesson of this experience. Defending my dissertation was a culminating experience, but the birth of my son was deeply meaningful in a way that the Ph.D. was not.

Advice from committee members

Brennan (2019) recommends that you be authoritative and confident. You are an expert on your topic, so you should demonstrate authority over it with the expected level of confidence. Failing the defence is rare, but you still need to perform on the day itself.

Jacobs (2018) reminds us that *"the bar that we set for ourselves is far higher than the one set by others"*. Another piece of advice that many have mentioned is to enjoy your defence. Your defence can be a very stimulating and rewarding discussion with experts in your field. It's a rare opportunity to get the chance to discuss your work with important researchers who've taken the time to read what you did (Vreede, 2016).

How to handle committee questions

Relation between defence format and questions

Your committee can ask a variety of questions. Depending on the defence format, your committee members may get to ask you just one (big) question, or they may ping-pong questions and answers with you for a considerable amount of time. In some cases, your committee members will want to go page by page. In some defence formats, one committee member has the leading role and will carry out most of the questioning. Understanding your defence format, and preparing for committee questions, as we discussed in Chapter 4, will help you get into the right mindset to answer committee questions.

Be prepared to defend your work without being defensive (Brennan, 2019). Acknowledge the weaknesses in your work and accept these – understand that the "future work" sections of your thesis and the discussion are appropriate places to address the limitations of your work, and recognize that sometimes research studies have some flaws.

Understanding the role of the committee members

Golding *et al.* (2014) conclude that most committee members have already made their judgement before the oral presentation on the basis of reading the thesis, and the defence will merely confirm their assessment. What their qualitative systematic review led to, is the development of 11 generalizations about committee member practices. Committee members tend to:

1. be broadly consistent
2. expect a thesis to pass
3. judge a thesis by the end of the first or second chapter
4. read a thesis as an academic reader and as a normal reader
5. be irritated and distracted by presentation errors
6. favor a coherent thesis
7. favor a thesis that engages with the literature
8. favor a thesis with a convincing approach
9. favor a thesis that engages with the findings
10. require a thesis to be publishable
11. give summative and formative feedback.

Committee members see themselves in two roles: 1) as gatekeepers, upholding the standards for a graduate degree, which is reflected by summative comments such as a final grade or evaluation, and 2) as teachers, supervisors or mentors, aiming to assist a candidate by offering formative comments, such as instruction, advice and guidance.

Surprisingly easy questions

When a committee member asks a question, the most important thing is not to rush your answer. If you find the question easy or trivial, don't brush it off too quickly. Take your time to answer it with the required level of depth, and address all parts of the question. When a question seems super easy, don't second-guess it. It's unlikely that your committee members want to ask you a trick question. There may be various reasons for an easy question:

1 for committee members to make sure they understand a basic premise in your work correctly,
2 because you didn't explicitly write something in your thesis on a topic that may, after all, not be so obvious for somebody who was not involved in the research,
3 because what seems easy and obvious for you, is not easy and obvious for somebody with a different background,
4 to warm up for a series of increasingly difficult questions in an exam-style defence,
5 to confirm you as the author of your thesis.

Not being able to answer questions

Not being able to answer questions during the PhD defence is one of the biggest fears of PhD students approaching their Big Day.

If you are giving a presentation, you will face questions at the end of it. If you are being examined, the exam will consist of questions by your committee members throughout the whole defence. In any case, you will receive questions at your PhD defence. This thought alone can cause a lot of anxiety and fear that you will be asked questions that you do not know the answers to. The fear of just sitting or standing there without knowing the answer can be paralyzing, and a lot of my (Olga's) coaching clients have shared that fear with me in our conversations.

So, let us discuss this issue. First, you are not supposed to know the answers to **all** questions you may be asked. If you do not answer one or two questions you can still pass your PhD defence. Your defence it not only about you, it is also about your committee members. They see this event from their point of view, and sometimes they want to show off their own knowledge in this area. Sometimes they may want to show that they have done the work of reading your thesis and preparing good questions. Sometimes those questions might be too difficult, and it is ok that you do not have an immediate answer. It has helped my (Olga's) clients to realize that there is an additional dynamic going on during the defence: between the committee members. Some of them might want to show off in front of others by asking clever questions, some of them might be trying to prove that they are good enough or knowledgeable enough. If you know this may happen during your PhD defence, it can help you feel more relaxed and comfortable. Shift your mindset from "they are going to fail me by asking difficult questions I can't answer" to "there is a dynamic of committee members showing that they have done their homework of reading my thesis, showing that they are clever and knowledgeable, and me demonstrating that I can explain the research I have conducted". That will help you feel more confident.

In my own PhD *viva* back in 2003 I (Olga) was asked by one of my committee members to derive an equation that was central in my PhD studies. I remember that I felt petrified standing at the whiteboard stuck halfway through the derivation. I also remember how they were smiling encouragingly and how they were asking me questions that helped me to get past the sticking point and complete the derivation. I felt they did not want to fail me and they understood that I was nervous and were willing to help me out. They saw that I had an understanding of the equation and they were satisfied.

When you get a question that you do not know an immediate answer to, it is ok to pause to collect your thoughts. You can repeat this question, asking for clarifications, you can write it down in your notes, you can take a sip of water, and you can even make a comment such as "it's a good question" (if it is true) or "thank you for addressing this topic". If you are giving a presentation and you are the only person who is using a microphone, it is actually useful to repeat the question so that everyone can hear. All these things can give you just enough time to collect your thoughts to give a good answer.

If the question is really tricky, it is acceptable for you to say: "I don't know the answer to this question". You can leave it like that or add some of your thoughts on the question. Just remember that not knowing the answer does not mean that you are stupid and do not know anything. It might just mean that the committee member asked a good deep question that needs further thinking and investigation. Giving them credit for this could be sufficient, even if you could not supply an answer.

Long and convoluted questions

Another difficulty with questions is that you can get one that is very long and convoluted. If you defend according to a format where your committee members each get to ask only one question, then you can expect long questions. The question may be laced with anecdotes and contain different sub questions. If you expect this type of question based on your defence format, go prepared. Take paper so you can make notes of the different elements that you should address when answering such a question.

I (Eva) remember the start of my defence as if it was yesterday and have many times mulled over the scene in my mind, wishing I had done better. My defence started with a very long question from one of the committee members from abroad. It contained three sub questions and was critical of the model that I had developed. While the content of the question was not unexpected, I was nervous at the start of my defence and I was thrown off by the length of the question and the number of issues to address in there. I didn't start off well. I was searching for words. I felt conscious of the fact that I am not a native English speaker. In hindsight, I felt like I rushed at the answer to cover all the elements raised and, worst of all, by the time I wanted to address the third element, I simply could not remember it. To my shame, I had to ask my committee member to repeat the third part of his question! What I should have done (and did for subsequent questions), was to take notes of the different elements of each question, sketch out the sub questions, and take a moment to organize my thoughts before I started speaking. In my experience back then, it was a hard question, but thinking about it later on, I realized that the content was not that difficult. I could defend the choices I made for my theoretical model and basic assumptions without difficulty, and I accept and recognize that, in my field of work, there are different opinions and that none of us have so far managed to get the perfect model. What made the question hard for me was simply its length, combined with the nerves I felt at the beginning of my defence.

Brennan (2019) also advises taking notes during questions:

- to help you understand the question better,
- to remember the questions, and
- to allow you to ask for clarifications where necessary.

In addition, having notes of the questions may help you make revisions to your thesis after the defence. Depending on the rules of your university, your supervisor might be present to take notes of the questions for you.

One thing to highlight here is that, while I (Eva) still regret how I addressed my first question, most of my friends, family and colleagues who witnessed the defence, said it went very well and that I looked calm and confident throughout. Nobody noticed that I struggled with the first question. You may be super critical of yourself and notice more than anybody else who is present!

Language-related difficulties with questions

During my (Eva's) defence I suddenly felt aware of my accent as a non-native speaker of English defending before native English speakers. In addition, if you have international committee members, your ears may not be accustomed to their accents, or they may use different terminology for technical terms than are common in your research group. If possible, have a conversation with your committee members before your defence. In this meeting, you can get to know their use of language and that can prepare you for the language-typical challenges you may face during the defence.

Carter (2012) studied the perceptions of the doctoral defence of non-native English speakers at the University of Auckland in New Zealand. Because the defence is a different hurdle for EAL (English as Additional Language) students, the search for best practice during defences is particularly difficult. The diversity of candidates in a globalized environment should not be ignored. EAL candidates face language-related anxieties before their defence, described as: "*the need to maintain the authority of a newly fledged expert in a formal, deep-level and consequential discussion*". The author also stated that "*Literature on formal interviews shows a mismatch of implicit cultural expectation to be potentially problematic to the establishment of credibility and trustworthiness*". The challenge for EAL students is to: "*…at the same time preserve a confident tone, and … not want to be seen as faltering while they perform complicated linguistic acts without rehearsal*". As such, "*the risk perceived by EAL candidates is that their linguistically grounded lack of confidence may prejudice examiners against them*". Besides these fears, the "*…darkest fear is that rigor might be edged with bias, a desire to keep what is alterior outside the gate*".

On this topic, Carter (2012) interviewed 11 recently graduated doctoral students. One of the interviewees mentioned that preparation for EAL candidates for the defence takes much longer than for native English speakers. One participant gained confidence when he reminded himself that although the examination is oral, it is not an English language test. This was summarized as: "*Language was a concern, but it shouldn't be.*". In terms of preparation: "*All participants had prepared for the examination by reading through their dissertation critically, looking for weakness. …/… Several rehearsed the question process*". In hindsight: "*Unexpectedly, given their success, all participants felt reflexively that their anxiety before the examination was justified*". This anxiety was described as providing a necessary impetus to read and double check, resulting in confidence. All study participants found the oral defence worth having as part of the doctorate and agreed that it was a rich experience. This conclusion is important, considering the cost and time involved in an oral defence: there is value in the defence, which is experienced as an extremely satisfying ritual of initiation and acceptance into the academic "tribe".

Advice from former PhD students

In the testimonies of former PhD students, we find the following advice for addressing committee questions. When you hear a question, you don't have to answer right away. It's ok to take a sip of water (Bright, 2016), take some notes, or, if the question is not clear, to rephrase the question and ask your committee member to confirm if you've understood it correctly (Newton, 2016) or to repeat the question (Trueman, 2018). It's perfectly fine to take a moment to write down the question, and sketch out possible answers before you reply (Newton, 2016). You can try to loosen up by pausing, smiling, and breathing deeply (Hassan, 2018).

Advice from committee members

In testimonies from committee members, we find the following advice for handling committee questions:

> Your defence is the opportunity to truly have an interaction with experts in your field. You can confront your work with the expertise of others, not only your promotor, and all this work will improve your thesis. You can consider the defence as a live discussion with the reviewers of your work, which is very valuable.
> (Debecker, 2016)

Van Vliet (2017) describes his way of examining as follows:

> One of the things I try to do in the *viva* is to push them to give me their views, and get them to speculate. My view is that they can speculate as much as they want, I am more interested in the reasoning used to get to their viewpoint, less in the viewpoint itself. If they want to claim that the moon is made of cheese, that's fine as long as they can come up with a convincing rationale. I also ask them to be critical of their own work, for instance by asking them to reflect what they would do differently if they had to do it again. And what I want to know is why they would do things differently. Also, standard questions are things like 'if we would give you 3 years of funding to continue this project, what would you do, what are the opportunities and why?' again pushing them out of the comfort zone and not just have them talk about what they have done. I want to see the academic capability and development, check their ability to take different viewpoints, show they have taken ownership of the work and were not just 'workhorses', and in a way, show pride in their achievements! Naturally there will be questions about the work itself, things to clarify, questions about the interpretation of results, etc. etc.

Remember that your committee is there to talk to you as researcher to fellow researcher, not to belittle you. If a question seems simple or ignorant, the reason is usually that committee members are simply interested in your research. *"Explain your topic with gusto, passion and love"* (Lantsoght, 2019).

If the defence format at your institution uses standard ways to address your committee members (such as "hooggeleerde opponent", "waarde promotor" etc. in the Netherlands), make sure you know how to use them. If you're confident using them, you can also use that time to think about the answer to your question.

Try to answer the questions to the best of your knowledge. Expect not only previously agreed questions,[2] but also genuine enquiries and questions that may arise in the moment during the defence. Even when there are set rules for the defence format, the committee members have the freedom to ask questions and take the defence in any direction (van Vliet, 2017).

Research insights

Trafford and Leshem (2002) analyzed one particular *viva* (from the UK) in detail. This *viva* involved five people: the candidate, two committee members (one more experienced than the other), the supervisor, and the Chair. The authors collected data during the defence, which lasted for 53 minutes. The supervisor wrote down the text of each question. In total, 36 questions were asked (five by the less experienced committee member and the rest by the more experienced committee member), and the candidate answered 47 questions as some questions had more than one element. These questions were plotted in a coordinate system with, on the *x*-axis, "Scholarship and Interpretation" and, on the *y*-axis, "Innovation and development in the research". For the analyzed defence, 20 out of 47 questions were situated in Quadrant D (high level in both categories), which indicates that these questions govern the assessment. While this research focused on one *viva* only, understanding the dimensions of scholarship and innovation can help you frame questions during the defence.

Possible difficulties during the defence

If you are worried about anything related to your defence, speak up. If you had no voice in the compilation of your committee and are faced with a lack of diversity, or uniformity of perspective among committee members, or anything else where you feel uncomfortable about your committee – speak up. Jacobs (2018) experienced a lack of diversity in her committee in terms of the perspective and background of committee members. She said: *"Had I been examined by a diverse committee, the questions would have been more diverse, there would have been an opportunity for a 'reset' with the change of examiner. I might have been able to recover"*. Raise your concerns with your supervisor before the defence and make suggestions for how to improve the situation (Jacobs, 2018). Gender, ethnic or research background diversity can help you feel more at ease during the defence and mean that you have a more balanced experience.

Make sure you have somebody on the committee (usually your supervisor) who is there as a person to support you. If you defend in the Netherlands, you are allowed to have two paranymphs (in addition to your daily supervisor and promotor in your committee). Having two trusted friends and colleagues flanking me (Eva) during my defence made me feel supported. As Jacobs (2018) put it: *"We all need advocates in the room, wherever we are. Knowing that you've got at least one person in the room who truly does 'have your back' is huge. Never go into an exam alone"*. This is however not always practically possible, for example in a closed defence format with only two committee members present.

Difficulties related to the committee

Doloriert and Sambrook (2011) show how, during the first author's defence, a committee member (an external member) was critical of her writing, which was an implicit criticism of her chosen methods. The author had deliberately retained a rawness in the early chapters of her autoethnography, reflecting her learning process, but the committee member insisted that the thesis should reflect only the final stage of her work. Such methodological differences may be hard to overcome and were the motivation for the authors to write a journal paper exploring methods further. Understand that such difference in opinion should be discussed by your supervisor with the committee. If you consciously made a choice to use a certain approach with your supervisor, the committee should be aware of that choice.

Horror stories and urban myths

It's common to hear defence horror stories when your defence is near (van Vliet, 2017): *"viva lasting 6 hours, external examiners with OCD discussing every comma, colon and semicolon, or the student being grilled about secondary school biology or chemistry that they have forgotten about long ago"*. This custom of sharing academic urban myths is part of the rite of passage that is the defence. I (Eva) remember people coming to my office in the weeks before my defence to share stories of their defences, how they managed to learn about the committee questions in advance, last-minute calculations requested the night before by committee members, and committee members not being able to travel as a result of a flight cancellation.

Sikes (2017) studied the topic of nightmare *viva* stories as so many of us have stories about disturbing experiences as committee members and supervisors, or accounts of what happened to friends and colleagues. These *viva* horror stories are the academic versions of urban myths. As there is no formal training for how to behave as a committee member during a defence, committee members draw on their own defences for guidance. Collecting experiences from colleagues, there seem to be five categories of possible problems during the defence:

1 committee members behaving badly,
2 supervisory issues,
3 thesis issues,
4 problems in the home institutions – issues around internal examining, and
5 student issues.

While Sikes (2017) did collect some shocking horror stories, the more common problems during the defence related to:

- having to disappoint candidates,
- apparently poor supervision,

- unreasonable fellow committee members,
- institutional relationships impacted by the assessment decision,
- students with unrealistic expectations or mistaken understandings of what doctoral study involves, and
- inappropriate uses of power.

Sikes (2017) explains these tendencies in terms of the increasing number of students doing PhDs, as well as the "perceived pressures" from university administrators and students to ensure that students paying high fees succeed, as well as the push from external bodies for students to graduate with shorter timelines. These factors have implications for the assessment process and for the committee members' experiences.

One of the respondents in this study mentioned: *"There are demon examiners but there are demon candidates and demon supervisors and dreadful situations as well and that needs documenting".*

When it comes to problems with committee members, one issue that arises is when the committee member seems to want the student to have written a different thesis and is not ready to acknowledge the one they have in front of them. This attitude can lead to questions during the defence that are unconnected to the work the student did. It has also been suggested that aggressive committee members are influenced by academic culture in general and gendered approaches to doctoral assessment in particular. Specifically, new methods such as auto-ethnographies, as well as feminist research, may be subjected to the biases of committee members.

In terms of supervisory issues, there are instances where the supervisor has not appropriately advised students or has not read their work, resulting in the submission of seriously flawed theses. Another difficulty is related to suspicions about the use of unfair means (such as plagiarism) and deciding how to deal with it.

Sikes (2017) also observes that the defence is not a neutral vehicle. The process is saturated with affect as a result of passionate attachments. The personalities of all involved in the defence, as well as their emotional states, will determine the process of the defence.

A major insight from Sikes (2017) is derived from analyzing the *viva* horror stories in the light of tendencies within the business world, where economic models attribute measurable and manipulative characteristics to each individual. The process of the doctoral defence, however, combines many more aspects than just scholarship. In sharing stories about the messiness and subjectivity of examining, and stories of personal uneasiness, we could move towards better practices for all involved.

Remenyi (2019) wrote a narrative of a defence where the candidate almost failed. The candidate did not prepare for his *viva* and did not have a mock defence. Before the defence, the thesis sat between minor and major revisions. How the candidate came close to failing his defence, and subsequently had to rewrite his dissertation over the next 15–18 months, was related to his behavior during the defence and the lack of goodwill from committee members, as well as the passive position of the Chair. Perhaps the small size of the room contributed to a wrong interpretation of the defence by the candidate – the room appeared cozy, instead of as a place for a serious examination. The defence was carried out according to the rules and in all fairness.

The first mistake the candidate made was that he was not able to answer a question about the central definitions of his work. He was also shown not to have been as careful as he should have been with some aspects of his research. His main mistake, however, was that in the second half of the defence, he forgot advice on how to answer committee questions and started giving very long-winded answers. He interpreted the defence as a jolly conversation and dropped his intellectual guard completely; he thought it was going well. The committee members focused on what was not in the thesis and did not work with what was actually there but the candidate should have taken the opportunity to show the strengths of his work. This problem could have been resolved if the Chair of the committee had taken responsibility for making sure that both the strengths and the weaknesses of the dissertation were discussed during the defence. While committee members' body language was friendly, they were nevertheless still examining the candidate. As Remenyi (2019) put it: "*no matter how pleasant, affable or warm the examiners appear, they are always examiners and the candidates' intellectual guard should never be relaxed until the results of the examination are declared*". This is indeed an important lesson to learn.

Advice from former students on difficulties

If you feel tension rising in the room, take a break to drink some water and change your approach during the defence. There's always time for a little reset during the defence (Imtiaz, 2016).

To make sure the mood in the room remains friendly, try to be friendly to your committee members and speak calmly and thoughtfully. "*The worst move you can make is to be defensive*" cautions Edwards (2017). Similarly,

Imtiaz (2016) recalls at one point wanting to defend every single small issue in the thesis. He recalls changing his strategy: he focused on defending the key sections and agreed to make amendments in sections that were of less importance.

Similarly, remember that the defence should be about your work (Newton, 2016): always bring your answers back to your dissertation. Newton (2016) wrote a little note before the defence that the dissertation is the primary source. The committee wants to evaluate whether the conclusions of your dissertation are well-founded; there's no need to show anything other than that. If you feel questions are taking you away from your work, return to your work and your dissertation.

Advice from committee members regarding difficulties

If you act as a committee member, be honest but don't be mean. *"Everyone can improve, but they don't have to be torn down and rebuilt to do so"* (Lantsoght, 2019). Van Vliet (2017) mentions that his first time as a committee member was exciting and sort of scary, but by now he enjoys defences, even though they can be hard work and not always fun. To summarize the role of the committee member, he states:

> In the end, it is important to realize that these examiners sacrifice time and effort, to give the candidates the chance to earn their degree. Even if we are not nice, let's appreciate the effort and remember these things once you become an examiner yourself!

In conclusion: "No matter the PhD defence format, you will learn, and you will be glad when it is over", says Coupland (2018).

Notes

1 Except in the case of "demon examiners", see section "Horror stories and urban myths".
2 If it is usual in your defence formats to know the questions beforehand.

References

Abboud, V. (2018). *PhD defenses around the world: A defense at Wayne State University*.https://www.evalantsoght.com/2018/10/phd-defenses-around-the-world-a-defense-at-wayne-state-university.html
Ames, R. (2016). *PhD defenses around the world: A defense in medicine from New York*. https://www.evalantsoght.com/2016/06/phd-defenses-around-the-world-a-defense-in-medicine-from-new-york.html
Brennan, N. (2019). 100 PhD rules of the game to successfully complete a doctoral dissertation. *Accounting, Auditing & Accountability Journal, 32*(1), 364–376. doi:10.1108/AAAJ-01-2019-030.
Bright, F. (2016). *PhD defenses around the world: A viva in New Zealand*. https://www.evalantsoght.com/2016/09/phd-defenses-around-the-world-a-viva-in-new-zealand.html
Carter, S. (2012). English as an additional language (EAL) viva voce: The EAL doctoral oral examination experience. *Assessment & Evaluation in Higher Education, 37*(3), 273–284. doi:10.1080/02602938.2010.528555.
Clarke, G. (2013). Developments in doctoral assessment in the UK. In M. Kompf & P. M. Denicolo (Eds.), *Critical Issues in Higher Education* (pp. 23–36). Rotterdam: Sense Publishers.
Corcoran, V. (2018). *PhD defenses around the world: A defense in medieval history at The Catholic University of America*. https://www.evalantsoght.com/2018/09/phd-defenses-around-the-world-a-defense-in-medieval-history-at-the-catholic-university-of-america.html

Coupland, K. (2018). *PhD defenses around the world: A defense in neuroscience from Australia*. https://www.evalantsoght.com/2018/02/phd-defenses-around-the-world-a-defense-in-neuroscience-from-australia.html

Debecker, D. (2016). *PhD defenses around the world: A defense in Belgium*. https://www.evalantsoght.com/2016/05/phd-defenses-around-the-world-a-defense-in-belgium.html

Doloriert, C., & Sambrook, S. (2011). Accommodating an autoethnographic PhD: The Tale of the Thesis, the Viva Voce, and the Traditional Business School. *Journal of Contemporary Ethnography, 40*(5), 582–615. doi:10.1177/0891241610387135.

Edwards, A. (2017). *PhD defenses around the world: A viva in linguistics at Cambridge*. https://www.evalantsoght.com/2017/05/phd-defenses-around-the-world-a-viva-in-linguistics-at-cambridge.html

Golding, C., Sharmini, S., & Lazarovitch, A. (2014). What examiners do: What thesis students should know. *Assessment & Evaluation in Higher Education, 39*(5), 563–576. doi:10.1080/02602938.2013.859230.

Hassan, M. (2018). *PhD defenses around the world: A PhD defense in Egypt*. https://www.evalantsoght.com/2018/10/phd-defenses-around-the-world-a-phd-defense-in-egypt.html

Imtiaz, S. A. (2016). *PhD defenses around the world: A viva at Imperial College*. https://www.evalantsoght.com/2016/04/phd-defenses-around-the-world-a-viva-at-imperial-college.html

Jacobs, S. (2018). *PhD defenses around the world: I passed and you will too*. https://www.evalantsoght.com/2018/12/phd-defenses-around-the-world-i-passed-and-you-will-too.html

Kamal, A. (2019). *PhD defenses around the world: A viva in linguistics from England*. https://www.evalantsoght.com/2019/05/phd-defenses-around-the-world-a-viva-in-linguistics-from-england.html

Lantsoght, E. (2019). *Advice for the PhD defense from examiners*. https://www.evalantsoght.com/2019/11/advice-for-the-phd-defence-from-examiners.html

Mallinson, D. J. (2016). *PhD defenses around the world: A defense in political science from Penn State*. https://www.evalantsoght.com/2016/06/phd-defenses-around-the-world-a-defense-in-political-science-from-penn-state.html

Mežek, Š., & Swales, J. M. (2016). PhD defences and vivas. In K. Hyland & P. Shaw (Eds.), *The Routledge handbook of English for academic purposes* (pp. 361–375). London: Routledge.

Newton, R. (2016). *PhD defenses around the world: A defense in California*. https://www.evalantsoght.com/2016/04/phd-defenses-around-the-world-a-defense-in-california.html

Remenyi, D. (2019). Never smile at a crocodile: A bad Viva Voce by the rule book. *The Electronic Journal of Business Research Methods, 17*(2), 67–73.

Ryder, N. (2014). Viva experience research, part 2: Some statistics. *Nathan Ryder*. http://www.nathanryder.co.uk/2014/10/viva-research-part-2/

Shimabukuro, K. (2018). *PhD defenses around the world: A defense from Literature at the University of New Mexico*. https://www.evalantsoght.com/2018/02/phd-defenses-around-the-world-a-defense-from-literature-at-the-university-of-new-mexico.html

Sikes, P. (2017). And then he threatened to kill himself: Nightmare viva stories as opportunities for learning. *Qualitative Research Journal, 17*(4), 230–242. doi:10.1108/QRJ-12-2016-0074.

Trafford, V., & Leshem, S. (2002). Anatomy of a doctoral viva. *Journal of Graduate Education, 3*(2), 33–40.

Trueman, C. (2018). *PhD defenses around the world: A defense in Northern Ireland*. https://www.evalantsoght.com/2018/02/phd-defenses-around-the-world-a-defense-in-northern-ireland.html

van Vliet, A. (2017). *PhD defenses around the world: The textbook pantomine villain? An external examiner's view*. https://www.evalantsoght.com/2017/11/phd-defenses-around-the-world-the-textbook-pantomine-villain-an-external-examiners-view.html

Vreede, B. (2016). *PhD defenses around the world: PhD defense in Portugal*. https://www.evalantsoght.com/2016/03/phd-defenses-around-the-world-phd-defense-in-portugal.html

Watts, J. H. (2012). Preparing doctoral candidates for the viva: Issues for students and supervisors. *Journal of Further and Higher Education, 36*(3), 371–381. doi:10.1080/0309877X.2011.632819.

7 After the PhD defence

Final graduation requirements

Fulfilling graduation requirements

Your final graduation requirements depend on your institution. There are different practices that exist around the world as described in Chapters 2 and 5. The first page of a thesis usually includes the following wording: "a thesis submitted in partial fulfillment of the requirements for the degree". In other words, depending on your institution, you may need to clear a few last hurdles before you graduate.

Typically, the fulfilment of most requirements takes place before the defence. You may need to think of:

- gathering proof that your paper(s) is submitted to or accepted by peer reviewed journals, if that's a graduation requirement,
- showing that you have taken the required number of credits for your doctoral school, if your PhD program has an educational component,

- compiling other documents that may be necessary to show that you fulfil all requirements to submit your thesis and/or for your defence.

After your defence, the final requirements typically come down to:

- obtaining the endorsement from your committee or the internal examiner after corrections,
- submitting your thesis to the official repository after approval,
- registering for the graduation ceremony,
- doing the paperwork to get your diploma.

Getting approval on corrections is common, among others, in the British system (Share, 2016), as well as in the USA (Lantsoght, 2011). In the UK, you will need to receive the endorsement from your internal examiner (Share, 2016) after implementing the changes based on the requested corrections. In the USA, it is typically the supervisor who approves changes after corrections. In Australia (Coupland, 2018), where the oral defence is replaced by a written review and response process, submission of the corrections plays an important role in earning your degree. Depending on the requirements of your university, you may need to provide an item-by-item response to the comments (preparing such documents is particularly important in Australia), or it may be sufficient to plan a meeting with the right person (supervisor, internal examiner, another committee member), show your changes, and explain your reasoning. Make sure you are well-informed about how you are expected to document the changes.

After getting your diploma, check if you need translations of your degree. If you are required to register your diploma in the country where you will be working, obtain the paperwork to get your diploma validated before you leave. You may need notarized copies of your documents and perhaps an official translation of your diploma with an apostille.

Distributing your dissertation

When you've submitted your thesis, don't let it just sit in the university repository. Distribute hard copies to colleagues. Mail them to collaborators internationally with a letter letting them know you have graduated or will graduate (you never know, they may know about a job opportunity that fits your profile). Take copies to conferences and hand them out. Besides conferences, see where else you can give talks about your work. Maybe a local high school or industry organization would be interested in an accessible presentation of your findings. Take some time to catch up with colleagues and friends – schedule appointments and take a copy of your thesis. Make some noise about your thesis on social media, and if your thesis is not under embargo, you can post it on websites such as ResearchGate, Academia.edu, and add the reference to Google Scholar, LinkedIn and your Orcid profile.

Practical tips

If your graduation ceremony has special dress code requirements, get your outfit ready on time. You may need an academic robe. Decide whether you want to hire or buy the regalia. If you graduate in Finland (Mikhailova, 2016), decide if you want to have your doctoral hat made by a hat-maker. If there are no special requirements, you can still see if you want to get yourself a new outfit for your graduation ceremony.

In the final weeks of your PhD, it may be wise to set aside some time to clean your office (Lantsoght, 2013). Even if you will stay in the same office after your PhD, go through all the stuff you've amassed over recent years and sort out what you still need, what you can pass on, and what is trash or recycling.

Make sure you update your CV. Add the project(s) you worked on, your updated educational information, your presentations and papers, and your service to the profession. You may want to make a general CV that lists everything you have ever done and then make summarized resumés for different academic, industry, and government jobs.

Celebrating your achievement

You have submitted and defended your PhD thesis, and it is a good time to celebrate it now! You have spent between three and six years on it, and if you have been doing it part-time, it might have taken up to ten years of your life. It's a big chunk of time, a whole separate chapter of your life. It is now time to think of a celebration that would mark the completion of this period of your career and life.

The "completion" of a PhD degree consists of several stages that can be spread out over several months in time, such as submission of your thesis, PhD defence, submission of your corrections, binding your thesis, graduation, and receiving the diploma at a ceremony or via post. While there are usually weeks or months between thesis submission and binding, there might be another six months or even a year until you can attend your graduation ceremony. So how should you celebrate something that is so spread out in time and requires so many steps at the final stage? Celebrate at every stage, in one way or another, for example by having a meal out with friends, or taking time off and doing something fun. Here are some suggestions and ideas for you to celebrate the various stages.

Celebrate your thesis submission by going out with friends for a meal or drinks so that you can finally relax and mark the end of a long, intense and stressful time. Going on a one to two week holiday is another good idea. The trip can be booked in advance and serve as a deadline and an incentive for you to finish writing and submit.

On reaching a milestone towards getting your PhD, or maybe at the very end of your PhD trajectory, you may feel sad rather than victorious. This is quite common: 42% of respondents of a poll on this topic (Lantsoght, 2018a) had the blues after their PhD, 41% didn't and the remaining 17% voted for "other, please explain". It also happened to both authors of this book. I (Eva) wanted to plunge straight back in after defending to write a journal paper, and I noticed I had difficulties concentrating and was feeling unexpectedly lethargic. I (Olga) also felt lost after thesis submission and even though there were only three weeks until the defence, a lot of that time was spent aimlessly, feeling low. Going on a holiday after your thesis submission will help you deal with the post-submission blues. You might not realize it now, but your work and life are only going to get busier from now on, and you might not have time for such an extended/relaxing vacation for a long time to come.

One of my (Olga's) clients from Croatia shared that she did not have a special celebration for her thesis submission but right after submission she signed up for the climbing club and going there every week, starting right after the submission, was a great way to mark the end of thesis writing. Having submitted your thesis is a good time to put your life "off hold", and signing up for a club or re-engaging in other weekly activities is a great way to mark this milestone.

The defence deserves its own celebration. In the UK, it is customary to have a little celebration right after the defence: there would normally be an email from a colleague or supervisor inviting everyone in the group to celebrate the new Doctor in a common area at the department. A bottle of champagne would usually be shared, everyone engaging in cheerful banter. It is also common to have a celebratory meal with the supervisor and a couple of close colleagues after the defence, and to meet at a pub at the end of the day with all colleagues and friends. The supervisor or colleagues usually buy drinks for the new Doctor who is celebrated throughout the evening.

In Germany, there is a tradition of colleagues making a special doctor hat and presenting it to the freshly defended PhD student. The colleagues create their own design that represents the PhD student's work. After the PhD defence, the whole group gathers and this unique hand-made hat is placed on the head of the new Doctor and lots of good memories and laughter are shared. In the Netherlands, it is common to have a reception in the university right after the defence, and then a dinner with committee members (if they don't have to drive back a long distance), colleagues, friends, and family at night.

If you are a workaholic and never stop to celebrate, you might be lucky enough to have your family or friends organize a surprise party or dinner for you, as happened for one of my (Olga's) clients from Singapore. She was busy working on thesis corrections while visiting her parents-in-law, and they set and decorated the table and celebrated together with the whole family and kids.

Right after or shortly after passing your defence you might want to spend a couple of hours doing the following: log into all your digital accounts, such as internet banking and utility and change your salutation from Mr., Ms. or Mrs. to Dr. Submit the change to your driving license as well. Do it as a celebratory activity and recognize the start of the new chapter of your career and life.

Posting about your completed milestone on social media, and receiving congratulations and cheers from your friends, connections and followers can be a good way to celebrate. This can certainly help you take in your accomplishment, even if you don't post on social media often.

In the Netherlands, the time from submission to defence is a continuum of meetings with committee members, making changes and showing them the new version of the thesis, arranging printing, and organizing the defence. For me (Eva), it took from November to June to go through all these steps. I took a post-submission holiday in November, and a few other weeks off during that time period, and I also traveled for conferences. But the big celebration in the Netherlands is the defence day, which includes the graduation ceremony in the same event. To mark this point in time, I (Eva) planned long in advance to do something memorable after the defence and graduation: in the midst of the chaos of moving internationally, my best friend and I escaped for a few days to go to a music festival in Germany we always had wanted to attend. I still have very fond memories of that trip!

After the PhD defence 185

Final recommendations

If you have read this book from cover to cover, congratulations on finishing it! If you are ahead of time for your defence, you can now start to dip back into it when you need it. Reread the part on selecting your committee when you reach that point, read the advice from former PhD candidates prior to your defence, and revisit the chapter on planning if you need to finetune your plan. If you are reading this book in the final days before your defence, take its most important lessons with you into your Big Day. Remember that you are the expert on your topic, try to understand your committee, and prepare accordingly for your defence.

In terms of planning for the defence, we've seen that the last months of the PhD trajectory can be quite different from the previous years. You have many more balls to juggle: arranging meetings with your committee (if you need their feedback and approval before the defence), finalizing paperwork for your defence, giving additional presentations about your research to let the scientific community know about the outcomes of your work, looking for your next job, and perhaps preparing an international move. Planning, keeping lists of what you need to do, and good time management become indispensable in those months. Include time for self-care in your planning, so that you can function optimally during that period.

The type of preparation you need for the actual defence is linked to the defence format. If you already have feedback from your committee members and your thesis is printed and final, then you should prepare for in-depth challenging questions of a global nature. If your defence is the first time you will have a thorough discussion with your committee members and you expect to make amendments to your thesis afterwards, then you may need a more detailed page-by-page preparation for your defence.

We have seen that there is a wide variety of defence formats around the world. The similarities between all forms of oral defences are as follows:

- It is your day to shine and celebrate.
- There is a significant emotional aspect to the defence that is always present, given the weight of the event. Take time to analyze your emotions and what you need for yourself in order to deal with these possibly strong emotions.
- All parties involved have the best intentions for the defence: you want to show that you are worthy of a doctorate, your supervisor wants to feel proud of you and confident of their judgement that you are worthy of a doctorate, your committee members want to show scholarship, and your Chair (if present) wants to show academic leadership. In most cases where professionalism trumps ego, none of your committee members come with the intention of harming or belittling you.
- You can expect to face challenging questions. You can take a moment to think through a question, take some notes (if the question is long), take a sip of water, and then provide your answer.
- The defence is an academic event and involves formalities. Whether these formalities are obvious, such as standard sentences used to address the committee members, or determined by each university separately (as in the United Kingdom (Morley, Leonard, & David, 2002, 2003)) depends on the defence format.
- The defence serves as an academic rite of passage, regardless of its format.

After the PhD defence 187

Understanding the differences between defence formats may help you understand certain questions or behavior from international committee members. Their understanding of the defence may be shaped by their experiences in their home countries.

This book is intended to be a toolbox. We have provided a thorough overview of different defence formats and advice from a variety of former PhD candidates and committee members. Since you are the expert on your research, we invite you to become the expert on your defence as well. As you go through your PhD studies and approach your defence you will not only master academic research skills. You will also need to become good at planning and time-management, you will need to enhance your academic writing skills and your oral presentation skills, as well as work on your emotional resilience. Your toolbox should therefore cover all those different aspects.

Every thesis, every doctoral journey, and every PhD candidate is unique. Therefore, we don't think a cookbook-style book serves all PhD candidates – there's no guaranteed "do this, and you'll succeed" approach. Just as a doctoral journey is period of reflection and deep thinking on a research topic, you need to put in the time and effort to gain the understanding you need to plan and prepare for your defence. You can work with the following questions:

- What is my working style like? What are the strengths and weaknesses of my way of working?
- How do I feel before and during stressful situations?
- How much self-care and relaxation do I need to keep a clear head?
- Which planning style and tools suit my needs best?

- What is expected from me during the defence? Do I understand the expectations completely, or do I need to gather more information? If so, who should I talk to?

You can build further on this during your doctoral journey. We invite you to become a master of your own work by reflecting on yourself and your working habits.

Further reading

Here are some references for your further reading per topic:

- Doctoral defences (Kara, 2016; Murray, 2015; Ryder, 2013, 2015, 2017a, 2017b, 2018; Smith, 2014) as well as the daily viva-survivors.com blog by Nathan Ryder (2020).
- General PhD advice (Farkas, 2008; Gill & Medd, 2013; Glasman-Deal, 2010; Iliffe, 2012; Kara, 2015a, 2015b; Lantsoght, 2018b; Mewburn, 2012, 2013, 2018; Peters, 1997, Phillips & Pugh, 2010; Rugg & Petre, 2010)
- Life in academia (Daly & Haney, 2014; Dee, 2006; Jahren, 2017)
- Productivity and planning (Babauta, 2016; Coyle, 2009; King, 2001; Newport, 2012; Rath, 2013, 2015; Tufte, 1990, 1997, 2001, 2006; Vanderkam, 2010).

References

Babauta, L. (2016). *Focus: A simplicity manifesto in the age of distraction*. Founders House Publishing LLC.

Coupland, K. (2018). *PhD defenses around the world: A defense in neuroscience from Australia*. https://www.evalantsoght.com/2018/02/

After the PhD defence 189

phd-defenses-around-the-world-a-defense-in-neuroscience-from-australia.html

Coyle, D. (2009). *The talent code: Greatness isn't born. It's grown. Here's how*. New York: Bantam.

Daly, I., & Haney, A. B. (2014). *53 interesting ways to communicate your research (Professional and Higher Education)*. Suffolk: The Professional and Higher Partnership Ltd.

Dee, P. (2006). *Building a successful career in scientific research: A guide for PhD students and postdocs*. Cambridge: Cambridge University Press.

Farkas, D. (2008). *The smart way to your Ph.D.: 200 secrets from 100 graduates*. Arlington: Your Ph.D. Consulting.

Gill, J., & Medd, W. (2013). *Your PhD coach: How to get the PhD experience you want*. Maidenhead: Open University Press.

Glasman-Deal, H. (2010). *Science research writing for non-native speakers of English*. London: Imperial College Press.

Iliffe, C. (2012). *How to get a PhD*. Iliffe independent.

Jahren, H. (2017). *Lab girl*. London: Vintage.

Kara, H. (2015a). *Creative research methods in the social sciences: A practical guide*. Bristol/Chicago: Policy Press.

Kara, H. (2015b). *How to choose your research question*. http://phdtalk.blogspot.com/2015/07/how-to-choose-your-research-question.html.

Kara, H. (2016). *Finishing your PhD: What you need to know. Know More Publishing*. Know More Publishing and Creative Technology (MicroDesign) Ltd. https://knowmoropublishing.com/

King, S. (2001). *On writing – A memoir of the craft*. New York: Pocket Books.

Lantsoght, E. (2011). *A PhD defense at Georgia Tech*. https://www.evalantsoght.com/2011/08/a-phd-defense-at-georgia-tech.html

Lantsoght, E. (2013). "Post-defense reality check: What should you do after defending your PhD." https://www.evalantsoght.com/2013/08/post-defense-reality-check-what-should-you-do-after-defending-your-phd.html

Lantsoght, E. (2018a). "The post-PhD blues." https://www.evalantsoght.com/2018/10/the-post-phd-blues.html

Lantsoght, E. O. L. (2018b). *The A-Z of the PhD trajectory – A practical guide for a successful journey*. Cham: Springer.

Mewburn, I. (2012). *How to tame your PhD*. Melbourne: Akimbo Productions.

Mewburn, I. (2013). *How to tame your PhD*. Lulu. https://www.lulu.com/

Mewburn, I. (2018). *How to be an academic: The thesis whisperer reveals all*. University of New South Wales Press.

Mikhailova, A. (2016). *PhD defenses around the world: A defense in Finland*. https://www.evalantsoght.com/2016/06/phd-defenses-around-the-world-a-defense-in-finland.html

Morley, L., Leonard, D., & David, M. (2002). "Variations in Vivas: Quality and equality in British PhD assessments." *Studies in Higher Education*, 27(3), 263–273.

Morley, L., Leonard, D., & David, M. (2003). "Quality and equality in British PhD assessment." *Quality Assurance in Education*, 11(2), 64–72.

Murray, R. (2015). *How to survive your viva: Defending a thesis in an oral examination*. Mainhead: Open University Press.

Newport, C. (2012). *So good they can't ignore you: Why skills trump passion in the quest for work you love*. London: Grand Central Publishing.

Peters, R. (1997). *Getting what you came for: The smart student's guide to earning an M.A. or a Ph.D.* Farrar, New York: Straus and Giroux.

Phillips, E. & Pugh, D. S. (2010). *How to get a PhD a handbook for students and their supervisors*. Maidenhead: Open University Press.

Rath, T. (2013). *Eat move sleep: How small choices lead to big changes*. Arlington: Missionday.

Rath, T. (2015). *Are you fully charged?: The 3 keys to energizing your work and life*. Arlington: Silicon Guild.

Rugg, G., & Petre (2010). *The unwritten rules of PhD research*. Mainhead: Open University Press.

Ryder, N. (2013). *Fail your viva – twelve steps to failing your PhD (and fifty-eight tips for passing)*. http://www.nathanryder.co.uk/fail-your-viva/

Ryder, N. (2015). *The viva: Who? What? How?: Frequently asked questions about the PhD viva*. http://www.nathanryder.co.uk/2015/04/the-viva-who-what-how/

Ryder, N. (2017a). *More than gold letters (Viva Survivors Blog Book 1)*. http://viva-survivors.com/ebooks/

Ryder, N. (2017b). *Per Scientiam Ad Meliora (Viva Survivors Blog Book 2)*. http://viva-survivors.com/ebooks/

Ryder, N. (2018). *Presents to the Future (Viva Survivor Blog Book 3)*. http://viva-survivors.com/ebooks/

Ryder, N. (2020). *Viva survivors blog*. http://viva-survivors.com/

Share, M. (2016). "The PhD viva: A space for academic development." *International Journal for Academic Development*, 21(3), 178–193.

Smith, P. (2014). *The PhD viva: How to prepare for your oral examination*. London: Red Globe Press.

Tufte, E. (1990). *Envision information*. Cheshire: Graphics Press.

Tufte, E. (1997). *Visual explanations: Images and quantities, evidence and narrative*. Cheshire: Graphics Press.

Tufte, E. (2001). *The visual display of quantitative information*. Cheshire: Graphics Press.

Tufte, E. (2006). *Beautiful evidence*. Cheshire: Graphics Press.

Vanderkam, L. (2010). *168 hours: You have more time than you think*. Portfolio, London.

Index

Note: **Bold** page numbers refer to tables and page number followed by "n" refer to end notes.

Abambres, M. 70
Abboud, V. 155
academic: ceremonies 14; credentials 75; fraud 128; judgement 151; practical/utility 101; research cultures 66; urban myths 170; verbal exchange 66
Addo, R. 110
advice: committee members from 156, 165, 174; former PhD students 154–156, 165
advisor/supervisor 6–7, 31, 57n1, 135
answer questions 159–160
anxiety 152; day of the defence 152, 153; defence anticipation 30; spur-of-the-moment anxiety 3; strategies for 153; students, face anxiety 9; thesis submission 59, 71, 101
assessment process 63, 148, 171

audience 85; former students 147; international audience 4; presenting for 82–85; public defence 20; questions 22, 55, 119
Australia 4, 18, 19, 54, 133

background/literature review 87
Bannister, F. 128
Belgium 15, 19, 119
best-case scenario 106
Better Presentations (Schwabisch) 95
Bible 13
bibliography 48
"big names" 75
Brennan, N. 61, 156, 162
British viva 28
Bulgaria 124–125

Canada 131–132
Carter, S. 163, 164
Championing Science 95
Chile 132–133

Clarke, G. 25, 128, 148
classroom setting 8–9
"cognate" member 74
collect data 44
collegiality 77
commencement ceremony 17
committee 10; assigned committee 78–79; committee feedback 82; external committee members 74–78; feedback 82; internal committee members 74; purpose of 72–74; selection of 79–82; user committees 79
committee members 76, 95, 168; advice for defence 147–148; and candidate 150; dynamic of 160; easy questions 158; role of 157–158; thesis submission 148
committee questions 3, 157; how to handle 157, 163; prepare for 95–101
Confirmation of Candidature 4
conflict of interest 76, 77
confrontation 76
consumer 151
contribution 97
Corcoran, V. 155
Coupland, K. 175
Covey, S. 52
COVID-19 pandemic 55
criticism 120, 155, 169
Crossouard, B. 30
cultural aspect, defence 30, 164

data analysis 66, 98
David, M. 63

Davis, G. 30
defence committee 80
defence formats 2–3, 10, 62; Australia 133; Belgium 119; Bulgaria 124–125; Canada 131–132; characterization of **116–117**; Chile 132–133; committee members prepare for 71–72; common format of 17; differences 27–29; doctoral defence practices 29–30; Egypt 136; emotional aspect of 10, 12; Finland 123–124; fixed schedule 22–23; France 120; Georgia 126–127; Germany 120; history and purpose of 13–15; important elements 15–17; Iran 135; Japan 134–135; Netherlands 118; New Zealand 133–134; Norway 124; originality 25–26; outcomes of 16, 61; Pakistan 135; plan and prepare for 7–8; Portugal 121; practicing for 109–111; public/private defence 21–22; and questions 156; Russia 125–126; schedules driven 22–23; similarities 23–25; single-step *vs.* two-step defences 19–21; Spain 121; student perception 29–30; Sweden 122–123; Ukraine 125; United Kingdom 127–129; United States 129–131; written documentation of 24; written/oral defence 17–19

"defences around the world" series 4, 5
Degtyareva, O. 43
Delft University of Technology 79
democratization 14
dialectical skills 13
differences 27–29
digital age 42
disputation 13
dissertation distribution 180–181
doctoral defence presentation 29–30, 188; background/literature review 87; conclusions 90; consequences 91; discussion 88–90; goals of 10; hypothesis 90; outlook 91; overview slide 87; prove hypothesis 90; results and analysis 88
doctoral regulations 9, 10, 16, 75, 79, 92; university 10, 11
doctoral training programs 127; full day session 11; half day session 9; instructors of 8–12
Doctor of Education (Ed.D) 14
Doloriert, C. 169
draft thesis 15

EAL (English as Additional Language) 163, 164
easy questions 158–159
educational information 181
educational reforms 13
Edwards, A. 173
Egypt 136
English language test 164
Engward, H. 30

enthusiasm 65, 150, 151
Europe 2, 29
European standardization 22
examination 66
examination time 27
examiner 6, 8, 17, 19, 21, 24, 26, 28, 29, 36, 55, 66, 72, 120, 121, 125, 127, 128, 133–135, 148, 169, 179
experimental method 41
external committee member 76, 77, 105
external examiner 120, 125, 127, 128, 135, 151
external reviewers 123
extra calculations 83

feedback 74, 78, 123, 125, 126, 128
female academics 30
final graduation requirements 178–180
final recommendations 185
Finland 22, 123–124, 181
fixed schedule 22–23
formative assessment 73, 111n4
France 120
full-time PhD student 37, 39
further work 98

generalizability 98
Georgia 126–127
Geraghty, A. 28, 29
Germany 36, 37, 120, 183
Ghent University 119
Golding, C. 24, 157
Go/No Go Meeting 4
Goulding, N. J. 28, 29
grading system 127
graduate research school 18

graduation ceremony 60, 184
graduation requirements 3, 15

Hay, L. 108
higher education 14
horror stories 169
hostility 76
humanity 146

ideal (clean) plan 47
Imtiaz, S. A. 128, 174
independent research project 76, 106
in-depth feedback 20
industry-oriented degree 14
integral component 16
intellectual property 100
interdisciplinary 81
internal examiner 127, 128, 135
international approach 4
international audience 4
international outlook 4
Iran 135

Jackson, C. 24, 76
Jacobs, S. 156, 168
Japan 134–135

Kabat-Zinn, J. 109
Kamal, A. 69, 154
Karle, E. 109
Killen, M. 70
Kuchner, M. 95
Kyvik, S. 77

lab assistant 37
language-related difficulties 163

Lantsoght, E. O.L. 14, 20, 23, 30, 35, 37, 38, 44, 86, 93, 104, 106, 118, 127, 128, 129, 167, 174, 179, 181, 182
Latin diploma 122
laudatio 60, 111n1, 118
lectio praecursoria 123
legitimation process 65
lekenpraatje 118
Leonard, D. 63
Leshem, S. 149, 167
library and digital copy 129
literature insights 4
literature review 98
Lunt, I. 25

making your presentation 6, 60, 68, 99
Mallinson, D. J. 156
Manidis, M. 110
Marketing for Scientists (Kuchner) 95
mathematical proof approach 86–87
meetings series **11**
"meetings with your coach" 6
methodology 98
Miguel, M. 63
minor revisions 27
"mock defence" 69; "trial run" 110; trial viva 125
Money, A. 128
Morley, L. 63

negative anticipations 66
Netherlands 4, 8, 15, 21, 36, 39, 81, 85, 118, 184
new and advanced methods 101

Newton, R. 174
New Zealand 133–134
non-verbal communication 149
Norway 124

observation 23, 66, 110
open forum 98
opening words 60
oral defences 14, 16–19, 24, 27, 36, 110, **116–117**, 186
original contribution 25
originality 25–26, 100; definition of 13

page-by-page preparation 186
Pakistan 135
part-time job 40
PhD/doctoral candidate 4–6, 108; former PhD candidates' experiences 42, 69–71, 110, 115, 154, 164, 165; part-time PhD student 37, 38
PhD funding 35, 39
PhD programs: defence planning 46–50; delays during sources 40–45; different types planning for 52–54; document 56–57; duration of 35–39; funding and duration 39–40; hard deadlines for 45–46
PhD research project 73
PhD supervisor 42
Phillips, E. 26
Pittman, C. 109
planning: PhD duration, hard deadlines for 45–46; PhD program duration 35–45; PhD programs, different types 52–54; research ideas to research planning 51–52; research journal 56–57; schedules driven 22–23; successful defence 35–57; towards your defence 46–50
Portugal 121
positive anticipations 65, 97
positive completion 2
postgraduate programs 110
post-submission 104
practical/academic utility 101
practical aspects 61–62
practical preparation 143
practical tips 180–181; formulas 93–94; practice before presenting 92–93; present often 93; recommend self-reflection 93; research question 94; take-home message 94–95; visual information 94
presentation 2, 4, 10, 161; advice 67–69; answer questions 60–61; audience, presenting for 82–85; defence elements 59–60; former PhD candidates' experiences 69–71; materials 99; practical aspects 61–62; presenting tips 92–95; research insights 62–67; skills 105; visual information 91–92; work summarizing 86–91
Price, D. 128

private defence 19, 20, 21, 132
Professional Doctorate in Engineering (PD.Eng) 14
professionalism 146
public/private defence 19, 21–22, 119
Pugh, D. S. 26

qualitative systematic review 158
questions 60, 130, 156, 187; language-related difficulties 163

recommendation 62
rector magnificus 118
Regal, B. 70
Remenyi, D. 128, 172, 173
research ideas 51, 62–67, 148
resubmission 17
Russia 125–126
Ryder, N. 148

Sambrook, S. 169
Schwabisch, J. 95
scientific literature 4
scientific method approach 86
scope 2–4
Share, M. 54
Shimabukuro, K. 69, 155
Sikes, P. 171, 172
Singapore 184
skills 66
social dynamics 150
South Africa 18, 27
Spain 121
speaking skills 2
special needs student 146–147

sponsorship 77
students: ignorance and misconceptions 67; negative anticipations 66; perception 29–30; positive anticipations 65; students plan 6–7; student understands 10; veracity and authorship 66
summative assessment 111n5
survey outcomes 29
Sweden 15, 122–123

"take home message" 87, 90
taxing relationship 105
teleconference 147
testimonies 4, 5
theoretical background 99
theories and theoretical frameworks 97
thesis submission 38, 101–103, 102–104, 148, 182; thesis defence 104–109
Tinkler, P. 24, 76
toolbox-based approach 6
Trafford, V. 149, 167
Trueman, C. 70, 145
Tufte, E. 95

Ukraine 125
unemployment 40
unethical practices 30
United Kingdom 2, 8, 15, 127–129
United States 2, 20, 37, 129–131
University of Berlin 13
"unpredictable moments" 110

unsatisfactory defence/oral examination 16
urban myths 169

van Vliet, A. 148, 166, 174
veracity and authorship 66
video conference 134
viva 2, 8, 23, 24, 28, 63, 69, 70, 72, 81, 96, 109, 121, 125, 126, 148, 151, 154, 160, 167, 170, 172; UK-style 2, 29, 81, 127, 149, 151

waarde promovenda 118
Watts, J. H. 24, 62–64, 75, 110, 148, 151
weaknesses 7, 10, 64, 157
Wellington, J. 65, 96
Westerbeck, Z. 109
worst-case scenario 105, 106
written defence format 4, 17–19, 18, 19, 27, **116–117**

You can heal your life (Hay) 108

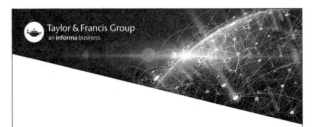